Monica Gribben

The Study Skills Toolkit for
Students
with Dyslexia

⑤SAGE

Los Angeles | London | New Delhi
Singapore | Washington DC

SAGE

Los Angeles | London | New Delhi
Singapore | Washington DC

SAGE Publications Ltd
1 Oliver's Yard
55 City Road
London EC1Y 1SP

SAGE Publications Inc.
2455 Teller Road
Thousand Oaks, California 91320

SAGE Publications India Pvt Ltd
B 1/I 1 Mohan Cooperative Industrial Area
Mathura Road
New Delhi 110 044

SAGE Publications Asia-Pacific Pte Ltd
3 Church Street
#10-04 Samsung Hub
Singapore 049483

Editor: Jude Bowen
Editorial assistant: Miriam Davey
Production editor: Jeanette Graham
Copyeditor: Sharon Cawood
Proofreader: Isabel Kirkwood
Marketing manager: Lorna Patkai
Cover design: Jennifer Crisp
Typeset by: C&M Digitals (P) Ltd, Chennai, India
Printed in India at Replika Press Pvt Ltd

Library of Congress Control Number: 2011945328

British Library Cataloguing in Publication data

A catalogue record for this book is available from
the British Library

ISBN 978-0-85702-931-7
ISBN 978-0-85702-932-4 (pbk)

Contents

Dedication

In memory of my Dad, Tommy – with gratitude for the values he taught me, the laughter he gave me and the love he left me. And with deepest gratitude to my Mum, May for always being there and whose many sacrifices and generous spirit taught me the true value of giving.

About the author

While living in Stavanger, Monica Gribben pursued her interest in dyslexia at Norway's Centre for Reading Research, setting her on a path where she would continue to be intrigued about the effects of dyslexia on individuals.

A graduate of The University of Edinburgh, Monica's background in languages and education helped her to explore the linguistic, diagnostic and psycho-educational processes of dyslexia. Specialising in support systems for students with dyslexia, she examined the support provision in Scottish and Norwegian universities. Intent on connecting theoretical with practical, Monica developed a study skills teaching programme suited to the learning needs of students with dyslexia, and from this the Toolkit was born.

Alongside her role as Dyslexia Adviser at Edinburgh Napier University, Monica established Dyslexia-Plus (www.dyslexia-plus.co.uk) which offers support to the wider community – individuals and corporate companies alike.

Acknowledgements

As with any project, there's you and then there are those who support you to make sure the job gets done!

Heartfelt appreciation goes to my editor, Jude Bowen for believing in my project and giving me this wonderful opportunity to give something back to the student population that has enriched my working life. Thanks also to the assistant editors who've guided and supported me at different points in this project – Amy Jarrold, Alex Molineux and Miriam Davey, and to the production team, marketing team and other staff members at SAGE who've supported my work each in their own way.

To my mentors who first introduced me to the world of dyslexia and who taught me well – Arne Løkken (Norway), the late Professor George Thomson, and Joe McDermott. With thanks to my family, friends, colleagues and the many students who've taught me the true meaning of dyslexia and afforded me the opportunity to say – I love my work.

Getting the job done has meant drawing on the wisdom and talents of others I knew would keep me right and tell me as it is. I am deeply indebted to my friend and colleague Fran McColm and my nephew Jonathan Stevenson for helping me unpack my ideas and for their invaluable and honest comments.

Then there's the creativity of 'min gamle kalosje' S.Christine Jensenius for her contribution to my front cover idea, my colleague Richard Firth for my Running Clock image and Jonathan for my Dissertation Diamond, Note Nugget, On and Off switches and W.Cube-It images. I am also grateful to the colleagues who provided assignment questions for use in my work – William Goodall, Lisa Watson and Richard Firth, and Dr Mike Sanderson.

Finally, there's the technology advice and support for my non-technology brain – thanks to my colleague Colin Gray and my friend Dr Panos Vlachopolous for explanations of podcast and vodcast software, my student, Keir McLuskey for developing the W.Cube-It into an Apps, and to my friend Bruce Darby for his guidance and support on my use of technology to ensure I did indeed 'get it right'.

How to Use this Toolkit

Don't like reading a book from cover to cover? Then this Toolkit is ideal for you.

Just dip in and out of the different chapters as and when you need them. Mix and match the tools – if one specific tool works for you then stick with it. It's all about you, your learning style and what works for you during your learning process.

A word of caution though about writing style and referencing when using the Toolkit. You'll see in Chapter 7 that I'm advising you not to use contractions of words when writing an academic assignment, and, of course, you'll see I'm using them myself throughout the Toolkit. Why? Well, it's part of my writing style so that my explanation of academic tasks and your understanding of them will feel less stuffy, and more accessible and manageable.

Different universities, courses and tutors use different referencing styles, even different versions of the Harvard system, so always check with your tutor the style they'd prefer you to use.

You can also go to the Companion Website for this book www.sagepub/gribben to access downloadable resources, all the activities from the toolkit plus a podcast for each chapter and to watch a video about the toolkit from the author.

So you're a student, you have dyslexia, you do things differently, and with that, you contribute to the world of education in an invaluably different way. So believe in your ability and enjoy!

If you would like a more accessible version of this book, SAGE would be very happy to provide you with a Word or PDF version of the text. Please email ebooks@sagepub.co.uk to make your request.

Companion Website

Video from Monica Gribben

Chapter 1 Podcast
Further web links for Chapter 1
Activity 1.1   Mapping Man: your worry – identifying, mapping, scaling
Activity 1.2   Reshaping your worries
Activity 1.3   Visual, auditory or tactile learner – or simply a bit of everything?
Activity 1.4   Styled learning
Activity 1.5   What's needed in your study bag? Complete your list
Activity 1.6   Your w.w.w.study space
Activity 1.7   Mirroring Janus – the worst and the best

Chapter 2 Podcast
Further web links for Chapter 2
Activity 2.1   Defining your goals
Activity 2.2   Name it to change it!
Activity 2.3   Scaling
Activity 2.4   So what's really stopping you?
Activity 2.5   Mirroring Janus
Activity 2.6   Advertising you
Activity 2.7   Name it, colour it!
Activity 2.8   Scale your feeling
Activity 2.9   Traffic light, all systems go!
Activity 2.10 Complete your Procrastination Mapping Man

Chapter 3 Podcast
Further web links for Chapter 3
Activity 3.1 Your lecture notes
Activity 3.2 Test your note-taking skills
Activity 3.3 Connections

Chapter 4 Podcast
Further web links for Chapter 4
Activity 4.1 Question – from word to meaning

1 Stepping out into University with Dyslexia

This chapter looks at the many worries you have about being a student, your learning style and engaging with the support available to help you get organised and manage your studies.

Stepping out, worries and all

Learning style – what is that exactly?

Get organised … more juggle, less struggle!

Assignments – organising

Your stepping out toolkit

Lightning ideas

Stepping out, worries and all

For most students, moving from school to university is a shock; it's sometimes even scary. From being a pupil in a class of 30, you suddenly find yourself as a student in a lecture theatre of 300, where organising and managing your own time and study is now your responsibility. There's no one telling you how long to study or what books to study, and there's no one nagging you about getting your homework in on time. It's all your responsibility now, and oh what freedom!

At first, coping with new demands and the new-found freedom to decide when, where and how you study can be hard and a little overwhelming at times, but somehow it will all work out. Just give it a little time and you'll soon settle down into student life. New things are always scary and hard at first for everyone. Remember, you're not the only new student; there are thousands of you, and, oh, don't worry about your dyslexia at university. You can't change the fact you have dyslexia. It's part and parcel of who you are, but it's only one part; it's not the whole of you. Just as being a student isn't the whole of you, there's a life outside of university. So make the most of your student days. Remember, it's only a few years in a whole lifetime. Enjoy it – the study, as well as the social aspect, dyslexia and all!

Don't make a big deal out of your dyslexia at university; don't let it stress you. Having dyslexia means your brain is wired differently. Think of a rabbit warren with all the furrows. Every brain has furrows; the dyslexic brain has extra furrows – maybe more, maybe wider ones. This means that when a message goes to the brain, it might go through an extra furrow and hit a different part of it, making the message scrambled. You just need time to sort out the message, to remember it and then process it.

Having dyslexia means you see things differently, learn things differently and do things differently – nothing more, nothing less. So, as a student with dyslexia you bring added value to the educational environment because you see the nuts and bolts of how things work, and all the bits in between. This is so much more than students who don't have dyslexia, and so your contribution is valuably different.

Remember, there's plenty of good support, as well as lots of strategies and learning tools to help you along the way. It's important to tap into these; that's why they're there. First though, let's take a step back, look at things right on the spot where you stand and figure out what's really worrying you about starting university.

Feel these worries are no different from your own right now? Not sure how to allay your fears? Scared your small worries will become huge ones and affect your chances? Remember, it's not so much about

I'm thinking I'm not good enough. That's all I ever heard at school and that's what I sometimes still believe. I don't want people to know I've got dyslexia because I don't want to be treated differently.

I'm scared. I tried Uni before and it didn't work out because I didn't know how to study. I'm scared I won't make it this time either.

I'm worried that my dyslexia will get in the way of things. I mean I've always been anxious about exams, of failing really, and I'm hopeless with organisation.

I'm worried about having to juggle my family life and my studies. Will it all become too much?

Activity 1.1   Mapping Man: your worry – identifying, mapping, scaling

Colour the worry bubble that you can most identify with. Now think of your own worry and where you feel it – sore head, wobbly legs, nervous tummy? Write or draw your own worry bubble and place it on the Mapping Man:

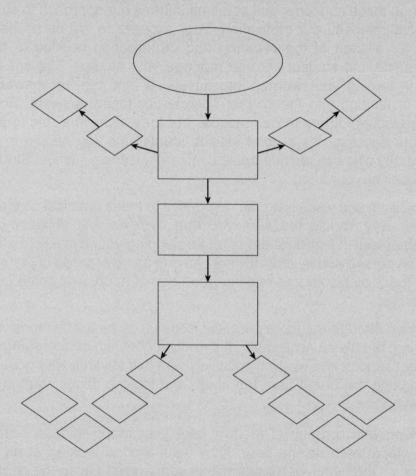

Scale your feeling. How did reading the worry bubbles make you feel?

Circle your answer:

anxious   upset   relieved   fine

How did writing your own worry bubble make you feel?

worse   awkward   encouraged   optimistic being a student and having dyslexia, it's more about what you do with it; how you manage your dyslexia and work with your worries that matters. One positive step is to take each worry you have and turn it into a question that can be answered. That way, it should seem less of a worry and more of a possibility.

Having worked with the worry bubbles, you'll see that we all come to university with different worries and concerns. Learning to work through these concerns one at a time informs our approach to study, our commitment, our motivation. Your experience will be no different. It's all part of the planning and organisation needed to help you settle into student life and manage your studies. The solution lies in turning your worries into questions that can be answered, and in tapping into the correct sources for these answers. Some are personal, others more practical, but they all have a role to play in your success. It's a good idea to identify the key people in the university who can provide these concrete answers, such as Student Services or your tutor.

Verbalising and visualising the responses to these practical concerns in this way should reassure you that dyslexia and university go together well. It's all a matter of understanding your dyslexia, believing in yourself and in your abilities, having an awareness of the support that's available and making good use of it; oh, and some good planning.

Working through the more personal issues may be a little more challenging, but it's all achievable. It's really a question of accessing the correct support and working positively with that towards your goal. It's separating the wheat from the chaff, and looking things squarely in the eye.

Working with a group of friends, take your Mapping Man worries and place them on the floor. Now walk around looking at all the worries. Does your worry seem less scary now? Given the choice, would you keep your own worry and work with that, or would you rather have someone else's? Discuss the worries, share ideas and experiences, and use the Mapping Man to record any solutions you've identified. Make sure you tap into the toolkit and any university resources that might be helpful. Keep your Mapping Man as a reference guide – from problem to solution. Take him on your study journey; add to his shapes to create a mini journal that records your experiences, strategies and solutions. This is your opportunity to write your own recipe for success; empower yourself!

♦♦♦♦ Activity 1.2   Re-shaping your worries

Working in a small group with other new students can make it easier to turn your worry into a question that can be given an answer. Place your worry bubbles on the table and categorise them into Personal and Practical. Now deal with the Practical section first; it's often easier to find concrete answers to the more practical issues first. Create a three-tiered flow chart of the practical issues to move from worry to question to answer. For example, let's take one of the worry bubbles above to illustrate the flow from one to the other:

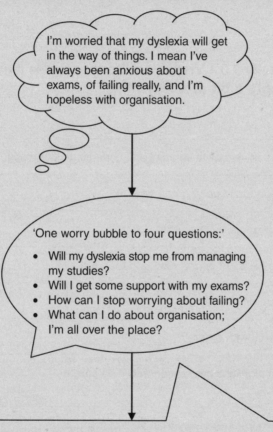

I'm worried that my dyslexia will get in the way of things. I mean I've always been anxious about exams, of failing really, and I'm hopeless with organisation.

'One worry bubble to four questions:'

- Will my dyslexia stop me from managing my studies?
- Will I get some support with my exams?
- How can I stop worrying about failing?
- What can I do about organisation; I'm all over the place?

'Four answers to four questions:'

- Your dyslexia will only get in the way if you let it; you're a student first and foremost remember!
- Contact Student Services, chat about the support you need, and find out what's available. Maybe some extra reading or thinking time in exams will help remove the anxiety.
- Fear of failure? All students have that. Get your support sorted and allay your fears. Still won't disappear? Then talk it over with your student adviser.
- Dip into your visual, auditory or tactile toolkit, use the organisation and planning tools that work best for you. Plan with a friend. Still struggling? Then get help from your adviser.

Learning style – what is that exactly?

We all have our own unique way of learning: specific styles, strategies, even rituals. What works for one, doesn't necessarily work for another. Some prefer doing things this way, others that. There's no right or wrong way, but the way you learn best is right for you. It's the style that comes most naturally to you, plays to your strengths, supports your learning processes and is specific to you as a learner; not simply memorising to pass an exam but learning to develop your knowledge. That's a learning style!

Activity 1.3   Visual, auditory or tactile learner – or simply a bit of everything?

Do you: ✓

use mind maps or shapes to connect and understand information?	
read information aloud so you can hear it?	
record information so you can listen back?	
use colours to highlight information and then read it?	
tap your fingers on your arm when counting?	
discuss concepts with others?	
use colours to highlight information and then create a picture or object?	
follow a mind map more easily than written instructions?	
use music or mnemonics to learn information?	
move around or walk when you're reading?	
see patterns in information?	
enjoy practical tasks that help you learn?	

Not quite sure of your style? Well, that's not so unusual. When something comes naturally, we seldom stop to think of it as a style. You've been doing it for so long that maybe it's time to give it a name. After all, moving from school to university means that you're moving from a more guided and structured way of learning to a more self-directed way. Knowing exactly what makes you tick and what makes learning work for you is helpful as you start university. That way, you can make the most of what's available in your toolkit and develop strategies that help to cement your study skills and your learning. Knowing your learning style will ensure that you'll use your time and energy more effectively, and what you learn sticks.

Want to know your dominant learning style? Complete Activity 1.3 and see Appendix 1 on the companion website for the answers and to calculate your style. Which one received most responses – V, A or T? Are you a bit of everything here but maybe one more than another? That's not so unusual. We all have a preference for one way of learning but quite comfortably tap into bits and pieces of other styles. That's why the style is specific to you! Still not quite sure? Want to test it out in Activity 1.4?

Which one did you opt for instinctively? Can you say why it was more inviting than the others? Then that's your natural style (see Appendix 2 on the companion website for the answers). So, if you've come out as a visual learner then you'll work best with the visual toolkit, likewise with the auditory and tactile. If you're a bit of everything, then dip in and out of every toolkit, working with the tools that you find easy to use, and stick with it. Implementing your own style of learning becomes more of a reality as you work towards organising and managing your time, meeting deadlines, passing exams.

Get organised ... more juggle, less struggle!

It's all in the planning, they say; get yourself organised and you'll manage better! How often we've all heard that. What's the big deal

 Activity 1.4   Styled learning

Choose a task to explain your experience so far:

- Write a letter to a friend.
- Design a poster or create an object.
- Draw a picture.

about getting organised? Just go with the flow, take things as they come. Yes, well, while that might work for some, it can be a complete disaster for others. It's not just about the planning. It's about juggling everything that's thrown at you as a new student, and working out where these things fit in your organisation box.

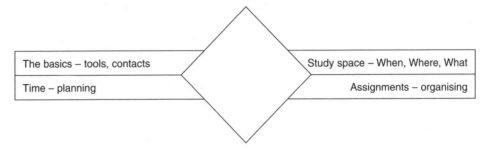

The basics – tools, contacts	Study space – When, Where, What
Time – planning	Assignments – organising

The basics – tools, contacts

Buying all the study tools you need for university might seem an obvious thing to do. After all, all students need to do this so they're ready to make a good start. How often, though, do we sit down to work and find we've forgotten our highlighter or left our notebook somewhere else? So the better organised you are at the start, the smoother your study periods will be. Good organisation is all a matter of looking at the bigger picture and working out the small things needed to manage set tasks. That way, you'll have less stress and more production.

Student Services

Arranging your exam and general support early on in your studies will make starting out in student life more positive and less pressured. It's easy to forget to arrange your support needs once you get caught up in the everyday demands of student life. As the demands increase, your dyslexic difficulties will be put to the test and maybe even exposed. So be wise – contact Student Services, find out about the support available and arrange an early discussion of your needs, including training on specific assistive software, proofreading or specialist study support. Once your support is in place and you start using it, student life will become easier to manage.

Library

Nowadays, lots of study information is readily available online; you're even encouraged to surf and search for articles. However, accessing information in this way doesn't suit everybody's learning style. Many students still prefer working with hard-copy texts in paper format. So

Activity 1.5 What's needed in your study bag? Complete your list

As well as the basics, you might need some subject-related materials and assistive software to support your specific needs. For example, a design student would need some sketch pads, a nursing student a medical dictionary.

Writing tools	Stationery	Organisation	Subject-specific materials	Assistive software
pens and pencils highlighters	Post-it notes notebooks folders	wall planner mobile apps diary	music score sketch pad medical dictionary	Inspiration Read & Write digital recorder

take at least 30 minutes at the start of your studies to get to know your subject section in the library – the place you'll spend a lot of time! This will make life easier, and save you running around at the last minute, struggling to find information when assignment time comes around.

Of course, there's the searching for information. Library catalogues – a language in themselves; all new and puzzling, and the bane of all new students' lives. So support each other; form a library group, devise your own catalogue, share responsibilities, resources and information. Create your group's own centralised referencing system by using a sorting and referencing tool from the toolkit. Need a kick start to understand catalogue language and find your way around the search engine or shelves? Then do yourself a favour – find out the cataloguing system used by your university library. Is it the Dewey Decimal Classification System or Library of Congress? Don't forget, the principle of finding information is the same – call number or letter (reference) = subject.

For example:

Dewey   Library of Congress

Table 1.1   System

Call number	Subject	Call letter	Subject
370s	Education	L	Education

The longer a reference, the more specific a section's subject. For example, a special education book on dyslexia by Gilroy and Miles

(1996) would be classified as 371.914 Gil (Dewey) and LB1050.5 Gil (Library of Congress) with Gil representing the first three letters of the first author's surname.

Know your section, learn the call number or letter and locating information should become easier. Of course, there's the decimal point. Confused? Then separate the decimal point from the numbers. Why not use your W.Cube-It (Activity 1.6) to devise a system that's easy to follow. Place the decimal point in the diamond and the numbers in the W-triangles at either side. Add additional referencing information in the other triangles – library? location? short loan? Or use your Mapping Man (Activity 1.1) if that's easier.

Still struggling? Then ask library staff to explain the system, show you how things work or help you find a text; it's their job – they're used to people asking for help.

Referencing? Yes, there's the referencing. It's vital to record the correct references when surfing, searching and gathering information. Knowing exactly what you've read and cited in your assignment makes it easier when dealing with the reference section, something we all struggle with (see Chapter 9). Haven't we all wasted time running around looking for a journal article or book because we've forgotten to fully record the source? Referencing accurately from the outset will make it easier to find texts again, particularly if you need to double-check information. Make this your positive practice, save your time and energy, and, oh, reduce the chance of plagiarism (see Chapter 9). Personalise your own system by adding to the list below.

Table 1.2   Personal system

What's the resource	Abbreviation	Where to find it	Abbreviation
book	B	university library	UL
journal	JN	national library	NL
article	A	department library	DL
electronic journal	EJ	electronic library	EL
blog	BL	reference section	RS
lecture notes	LN	short loan	SL
academic poster	AP	personally owned	your own initials
pamphlet	P		

If keeping a hard-copy notebook of your sources, strategically place Alpha-colour labels (see Table 1.3) to make it easier for you to record and locate references. Likewise, colour-code electronic information.

Activity 1.6   Your w.w.w. study space

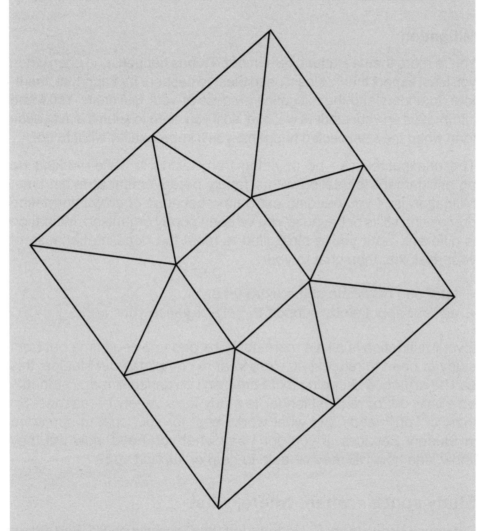

Place your choices in the W.Cube-It:

When do you work best? Morning, afternoon, evening? Where are you most productive? At university: library, study room, computer suite? At home: bedroom, kitchen, study area? What motivates you most? Working alone, in pairs, in groups?

Table 1.3 Alpha-colour

red	a b c	orange	o p q r
yellow	d e f g	purple	s t u v
pink	h i j	blue	w x y z
green	k l m n		

Mitigation

You're more than a student, remember. Things happen, and often when you least expect them or least need them to happen. It's important, therefore, to understand the mitigation process at your university. You'll find information on your student website, so if you need to submit a mitigation form when the unexpected happens, you'll know exactly what to do.

The unexpected can be anything from taking ill while working on an assignment to dealing with a family bereavement at exam time. Mitigation isn't you needing extra time because of slow information processing skills or because you've been poorly organised. Mitigation is different. So if you're struggling to meet the deadline because of your dyslexia, then chat to your:

- tutor and negotiate some extra time
- adviser about study support to help organise your work.

If your mitigation is a little more complex and you need time out from study or need to request an extra year to complete your studies, this can be arranged. Needing extra time isn't so unusual; many students take time out or request longer to study for a variety of reasons. So think of your needs and what works best for you; chat to someone in Student Services. If you don't say what you need, how will they know, and how will they be able to help or support you?

Study space – when, where, what

Put your worries to rest? Understood your learning style? Sorted out the basics of your support, your working tools and your key contacts? Now it's time to work out your w.w.w.: when, where, and what makes you motivated to study.

We all have our preferences, let's face it. Some like to work alone in the peace and quiet of the library early in the morning, others late into the night in their student flat, music blaring in the background and papers spread out around them on the floor. Maybe even in a group. Does it really matter? Of course not! As long as the study space works for you.

Sometimes you'll stick to the same space, other times you'll need to change it and for different reasons. Perhaps it's the project you're working on or the group you're working with that requires a different study space. Don't stress about changing it to suit different needs. However, if your regular study space isn't working for you, then, most likely, neither are you. Why not change it? Change your space, change your production rate.

Time – planning

New life, new structure and so much time, or so it seems. Remember, it's your responsibility now, so make it work for you. Good time management needs careful planning and organisation of both your personal and student life. Allocate time for family, social and work commitments, as well as study periods. Factor in your surfing and searching time, your reading, annotating and writing-up time. Plan and organise your time around ongoing lectures, tutorials or group projects. Give some structure to your day and allow your confidence as a student to grow and develop. Soon, the worries you came with will disappear.

Assignments – organising

It's true! You're generally not given an assignment as soon as you start university, but it won't be long before the first one comes along, and then the second, and maybe even another at the same time. As you're studying more than one subject, you'll soon find assignments pile up and, oh, the struggle trying to juggle. How will you manage it all, we hear you say?

Stop here, think back to your school assignments and how you worked your way through these. Think of the times you planned them or didn't plan them and the consequences of each. Which seemed to work better for you? Be aware! University assignments are much larger and much more demanding than anything you've done before. There's more reading, more organisation, more critical thinking, more discussion, more writing, and, oh, more referencing. So with previous experience in your pocket, move forward wisely and start planning ahead. Draw up a basic plan – organise your time, your assignment folder, your notes, your task, your student life.

The 'planning' building blocks

Planning and organising your assignment folder gives value to what you do, and saves time and energy later. Electronic folder or hard copy – choose what works best for you. The same planning principles apply to each. For the electronic folder, use a mind-mapping tool.

- separate different assignment topics using dividers
- write the topic's name on the edge of the divider

- keep a plan of your assignment at the front of the folder
- put your assignment timetable on the front inside cover of the folder
- put your 10-step assignment checklist on the back inside cover of the folder (Chapter 7)

- keep your revision notes and articles in plastic wallets
- write the topic's name on a sticker and place on the bottom right-hand corner of the plastic wallet

- keep a separate section for the printed copy of your assignment while editing
- keep a references and bibliography section; add to this as you progress

- discuss the expectations of your assignment with your tutor
- timetable your research and writing-up time; take account of your other commitments and your 'me' time

The 'not planning' downward tunnel

Not planning your studies can lead you through a downward tunnel that results in ultimate failure.

Having worked through your worries about starting university with dyslexia, worked out your learning style, addressed your support needs, and organised yourself, life as a student should seem more positive now. Not convinced? Need more encouragement? Then look at Mirroring Janus in Activity 1.7.

Which situation seems most favourable? It's your choice.

- making excuses for not getting started
- procrastination setting in

- thinking about how others are doing
- worrying about how you're doing

- failing to take regular breaks
- skipping classes because you need time to complete your assignment

- working at your least productive times because of looming deadlines
- losing valuable marks because of late submissions, or failure to make tutor contact when you're struggling

- having insufficient lecture notes for your assignments (or exam revision) because of those skipped classes
- lacking sufficient exam revision time because you need extra time to complete your assignment

- struggling with a backlog situation
- experiencing anxiety
- feeling stressed
- worrying about potential failure

Activity 1.7 Mirroring Janus – the worst and the best

Make a note of the best thing that could happen to you, if you remain organised and manage your studies. Then make a note of the worst thing that could happen, if you don't manage.

Worst   Best

_____   _____
_____   _____
_____   _____

Your stepping out toolkit

The stepping out toolkit is designed to help you settle into university life, set your worries aside and build your confidence as an independent learner. There's something for all of you in the toolkit, regardless of how you like to learn or how confused you feel when you first walk through the university doors. Remember to check out Appendix 7 on the companion website to see how these tools operate.

The visual learner's stepping out toolkit

This toolkit lets you see things as you plan and organise your student life. By using pictures or diagrams, you'll soon see the bigger picture, and all the nuts and bolts of university life. That way, you should see the possibilities in the different contribution you bring to the educational environment. Things should seem less scary!

- Bubbl.us
- Coloured stickers and Post-its
- Dabbleboards
- Inspiration
- Mapping Man
- Mind Genius
- MyWebspiration
- Noticeboard
- Personal reference system
- Sticky text highlighter strips
- Storyboarding
- Topicscape
- Wall planner
- W.Cube-It

The auditory learner's stepping out toolkit

Need to hear things so you understand better? Then this toolkit offers opportunities to talk things over, to hear things aloud and to think things through. It allows you to integrate what you hear with what you think and how you approach and manage tasks. Engaging with your educational environment should be smoother.

- Background, relaxation music
- Calendar
- ClaroRead
- Diary
- Digital recorder
- Journal
- Library support
- Mentoring or buddy system
- Mobile A to Z organiser
- Mp3
- MyStudyBar
- Notebook
- Read & Write
- Stress management
- Student Adviser
- Study log
- Turnitin

The tactile learner's stepping out toolkit

Enjoy doing things while trying to learn? Feel this helps information 'stick' better? Then the tools in this toolkit will allow you to develop strategies that support your specific learning style. Working comfortably with these tools should reinforce your learning process and give value to your educational contribution.

- Background, relaxation music
- Coloured labels
- Highlighters
- Mindfulness exercises
- Mini reflective journal
- Stress ball
- Subject-related online activities
- Study Buddies bookmarks
- Wobble board
- Worry stone

 ## Lightning ideas

- Find answers to your worries and box them
- Work out your learning style and stick to it
- Match your learning style with your toolkit
- Remember your personal w.w.w. study space
- Remember the 'me' times in your timetable
- Take one day off, free from study, to recharge your batteries.
- Don't study for more than 45 minutes at a time
- Take at least 30 minutes early on in your student life to know your library section
- Contact Student Services, find out about the support available and arrange an early discussion about your support needs
- Engage with your support
- Check your study bag has all you need
- Leave your worries at the door and step into your new learning environment with new-found confidence
- Believe in your abilities!

Different learning style, different educational contribution

 Please go to the Companion Website for this book www.sagepub.co.uk/gribben to access downloadable resources, all the activities featured here and a podcast for this chapter.

2 Procrastination

This chapter looks at the 'tomorrow never comes' habit by taking you through the five-step Getting into Gear Process involved in facing your procrastination habits and in breaking the mould.

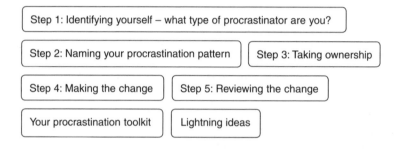

Step 1: Identifying yourself – what type of procrastinator are you?

Step 2: Naming your procrastination pattern

Step 3: Taking ownership

Step 4: Making the change

Step 5: Reviewing the change

Your procrastination toolkit

Lightning ideas

Procrastination – what is it exactly?

Procrastination is the art of putting things off; of delaying the inevitable. Instead of dealing with tasks as they come along or learning to prioritise, a good procrastinator will find a believable reason for putting things off until tomorrow. Don't be mistaken though – procrastinators seldom sit around doing nothing. They're always busy, but with the wrong things.

It's easy to make excuses for avoiding doing what really needs to be done. Students are often the worst procrastinators, especially when faced with more than one assignment at a time, and having to juggle both the researching and the writing up. It can often become worse when the demands of family life, and all the stresses that come with that, also have to be juggled. Student life can become complex and remaining motivated, well – 'what's that?', you say after a while.

When you procrastinate, you're only delaying the obvious – putting off working on your assignment. Procrastination doesn't get your work done for you nor does it make it disappear. It merely delays the working process and often makes it harder to get motivated as time goes on. Any assignment you have will still be there the next day, and the day after that, and every other tomorrow until you step out and break the mould. The longer you procrastinate, the harder it is to get into gear, and the higher your anxiety level rises. Suddenly, you find yourself stuck and not knowing quite which way to turn or what to do. It's quite simple really; you can either keep the habits or change the behaviours – the upwards or downwards response. What's it to be then? Think, choose and be honest with yourself!

The five-step getting into gear process

Procrastination is something you've practised over a lifetime, so it won't disappear overnight. Remember, getting yourself motivated again will be hard work, particularly if lots of different issues are going on at the same time, and the pressure builds up.

Working your way through these five steps will test your belief about your motivation and commitment, forcing you to face your fears and move out of your comfort zone. By doing this, you should be able to make the changes necessary so that you don't just 'talk the talk' but also 'walk the walk'. When dipping in and out of the toolkit, ask yourself:

- Why do you keep putting things off, and what are the consequences of that?
- What stops you from getting things done?
- How can you break the mould and get into gear with some practical, easy-to-use strategies?

Remember, things don't have to be exact or precise; there's always room for revisiting and reworking things. Just be honest in your responses and you'll get there.

Step 1: Identifying yourself – what type of procrastinator are you?

The first step in this process is to be clear about the part of you that's the procrastinating student. Are you a natural procrastinator or are some of the worries addressed in Chapter 1 still lurking in your worry bag and affecting your thinking? Be clear about why you want to study and what you hope to achieve. Write this down, read it, visualise it and remember it. Let it define your learning.

Activity 2.1   Defining your goals

What do you want to achieve?	
What do you need to do to get there?	
How do you plan to get there?	
Who will help you along the way?	

When you look at your goal written down in black and white, how do you feel? Do you believe it's achievable? Or has negativity taken a hold of your self-belief? Remember, you're not alone as a procrastinator or as a student who needs a little kick-start. Lots of students are in the same boat. The point is that to move from procrastinate to motivate, you need to want to change and commit to it. If you're fed up with being stuck, then maybe it's time to make that move.

 Case Study: Ryan, aged 22, final-year marketing student

'I was just settling into doing some work on my honours project. I'd got some books from the library and needed to finally start working my way through these, as my deadline was only three months away. The practical bit was done, it was just the theory I needed to sort out. After all, I'd put off getting started long enough. Anyway, I'd just about started when my friend called, inviting me to a barbeque. Naturally, I dropped the books, jumping at the chance of a free feed. Oh, I'll make a start tomorrow, I thought.

The barbeque went on for longer than expected and I arrived home very late feeling rough, after having had more than a few drinks. I slept late the next morning and, as I'd a dental appointment late on in the afternoon, I decided to leave things until tomorrow again. After all, who can concentrate after having a filling? Another day gone with no work done! ... and so the story goes on. I simply kept putting things off, finding it even harder to get started.'

With hindsight, is there anything Ryan could have done differently? Being a final-year student, do you think he should have learned to prioritise, organise and plan better? What about reading and writing much earlier? What about his stress levels now? How will that affect his performance? What advantages would he have had in saying 'no' to the barbeque or to drinking so much?

Admitting that you procrastinate and how often you put things off is useful, but being able to say what type of procrastinator you are should help identify a specific support strategy. For example, if you're a Stresser and an Avoider then working with a Student Adviser on your procrastination habit is a positive way forward.

As well as giving you some stress-management strategies, your Adviser can help you get to the root of why you avoid getting started. By using your toolkit, you can map out the connections in the different stages of your 'Avoider' pattern. Do you avoid getting started because you don't know how to write in an academic style, or do you have a longstanding fear of failure?

Activity 2.2   Name it to change it!

Ever found yourself in a similar situation to Ryan? Who hasn't! Start charting your progress and ask yourself honestly:

What are the consequences of this? Where do you think you're at now? Do you keep going as you are, going it alone or do you need that kick-start to break the mould? Are you stuck with the negative or can you move forward towards the positive? What can you change?

Seeing a picture of your situation unfold with the help of your toolkit should make it easier for you to answer those questions, and to see whether you can get into gear and commit to change.

Do – when?	Name it to change it	Done – when?
this week	plan assignment; work back from deadline date	...../...../....
		...../...../....

Activity 2.3   Scaling

Where do you fit on the procrastination scale? Circle your answer.
Are you someone who puts things off:

all the time   most of the time   sometimes   hardly ever   not at all

If you've ticked more than one of the types in Table 2.1, then it's time to get in touch with the things that are blocking you.

Step 2: Naming your procrastination pattern

The next step in seeing the bigger picture is being able to work out your pattern and add to it or even subtract from it. Look honestly at the things that are stopping you, even blocking you, and how you feel about that. Activity 2.4 should help you put a name to your habits.

Table 2.1   Procrastinator types: which are you?

Type	Description	✓
worrier	• constantly fret about not managing • constantly worry about failing	
stresser	• use up so much energy stressing about the task that you find it hard to focus and get going	
avoider	• believe the task will go away or do itself, so you avoid thinking or doing anything about it	
excuse-maker	• keep making excuses for getting started or for not getting started	
putter-offer	• do any other mundane task rather than what you actually should be doing	
dreamer	• constantly dream about being finished but never do anything about getting started so you can get to that point	
over-doer	• gather too much information, take on too much and then can't see the wood for the trees	
unmotivated	• can't be bothered • not at all interested	
perfectionist	• never seem happy with what has been produced • go over and over things hoping to make it all perfect	
lazy	• can't be bothered even thinking about the task, never mind doing anything to get started	
pessimist	• so afraid of getting it wrong and failing believe you'll get it wrong and fail	
over-loader	• have difficulty saying 'no' and so take on too much and feel overwhelmed with tasks	

Activity 2.4   So what's really stopping you?

Things that stop you	(√)
fear of failure	
thoughts of getting started	
beginning the task	
making decisions	
keeping going	
completing the task	
taking time out	

Name it, shape it!
How does this make you feel?

What are your thoughts about it all?

What's really blocking you?
Can you say why?

Taking your current assignment, have you asked yourself the why, how and what questions, and worked out the consequences of all that? What's the most challenging thing about this pattern and your study approach? How does it affect your confidence and belief in your own ability in getting your thoughts down on paper? Why does it shape the way you work or the way you gather information, think things through, examine, rationalise or conceptualise things, or even define your learning? Lots of questions, I know, but they'll help you get to the root of why you're struggling with this assignment.

Can you sketch your current experience? Remember, it doesn't have to be perfect; matchstick men, shapes or symbols are fine – as long as it says something

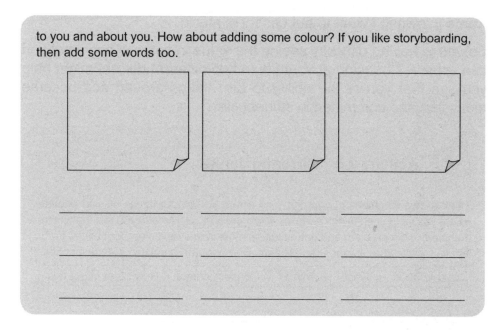

to you and about you. How about adding some colour? If you like storyboarding, then add some words too.

Now that you've moved a little way forward in the five-step process, check out your toolkit again and see how things are unfolding. Read your story out loud; listen to it, hear it, share it with someone you trust. Does it seem more real to you now? Do you feel ready to move forward and take ownership of your procrastination? Or do you need to ask yourself again why you're doing this?

Step 3: Taking ownership

Procrastination is a habit that happens for a variety of well practised reasons. Taking ownership means that you:

- admit to habitually putting things off
- have identified and named your procrastination habit
- have a general picture of your student life as a procrastinator
- want and need to change.

Continually putting things off or waiting until your stress level becomes almost unmanageable creates a negative pattern that can be difficult to break through. What you're actually creating is a failure to see the value in yourself and in your abilities. At times, you may lose sight of the best in yourself and all the valuable qualities you can bring to your student life. If you're seeing a more negative than positive picture of how you function as a student, then it's time to take that next step, and take ownership of your 'tomorrow never comes' habit.

Name it, own it! I want to but can't, I'm stuck!

So you're having difficulty seeing the value in yourself and what you can achieve? Looking at your life in two different mirrors might help you see that you've the ability to turn things around and become motivated and committed in student life.

Activity 2.5   Mirroring Janus

Think of two situations in your life: one where you've put things off and another where you've tackled things head on. Mirroring Janus will make you see that you're both part of the problem and part of the solution in this next step. Just as the problem lies within you, so does the solution. Be open and honest in your responses.

What I put off	What I tell myself	Consequences	How I feel about this

What I tackle	What I tell myself	Consequences	How I feel about this

Doodle the difference in your mirror responses – your life situation, attitude, goals, support, reward? More confidence, less stress?

What about your current assignment? Your problem, your solution – doodle it! What can you do differently?

Problem		Solution	
Consequences		Consequences	
How you'd feel		How you'd feel	

Can you now see the more favourable Janus? What's your choice – the put off or the tackled? Which one causes less anxiety and more harmony? Think of your goals and what you need to do to get there! When looking at the pattern that's unfolded, can you honestly say what you're really procrastinating about and why? Is it as scary as you first thought? Or do you think with a little helping hand, you'll manage? What's it to be? 'Talk the talk' and all the negatives it brings – the disinterest, de-motivation, fear of failure, lack of confidence, poor self-belief, poor focus, fatigue, anxiety, pessimism, low mood? Or do you now feel ready to 'walk the walk' and commit to self-belief and self-motivation, and move forward with all the positives it brings – confidence, self-esteem, balanced study, relaxation time, good grades, success?

If you're still having difficulty, then look back to Activity 1.1 and your responses, and review your basic planning and organisation (Chapter 1). Have you missed something out? Does it need to be revised in any way so that you can finally take ownership of your procrastination? If so, do it now!

Now that you're halfway through the Five Steps, can you see what's changed in the process – you? ... how you feel? ... how you think? Are your dyslexic difficulties blocking you? Are you generally not managing your assignments, or is there something more going on in your personal life?

 Activity 2.6   Advertising you

Still struggling to think of the best in you? Okay, think! If you were an advertisement, how would you sell yourself? You're the latest gadget on the market and everyone wants one. What 'value for money qualities' do you possess? Working alongside a friend, jot down your 'value qualities' and convince the market! It's often easier for others to see your values and gifts, and give a different dimension to your story. Hearing your story verbalised is positive; the valuable will stick and you'll become unstuck.

Taking ownership means it's important to squarely look at what's going on round about you, to face your fears and to get the support you need to move forward. Otherwise, you're on a fast track to the downward spiral.

Or halfway through, does it seem more positive, more manageable and achievable? Has it been worthwhile? What have you learned about yourself from the process so far? Remember the positive! It's easy to let the negative overshadow how you feel about yourself and about your student life in general. Think of one positive thing that's forced you to take ownership; name it and box it. Are there any other skills you need to learn or other issues you need to deal with before moving forward to make the change?

Step 4: Making the change

With that done and having worked your way through some of the Steps, can you now draw up a plan of how you intend to achieve your goals? Change your habits? Make things work?

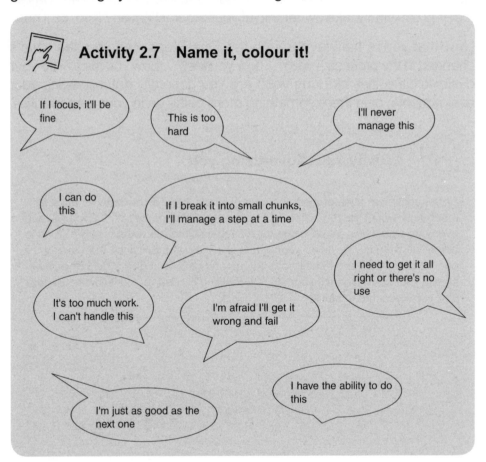

Feel you're ready to make the change? Then test your self-belief. Which bubble seems most familiar to you? Which one honestly explains how you're feeling at this point?

Have you chosen a positive or negative thought bubble? Do you feel comfortable with your choice? How far have you come along the way?

Making the change means leaving behind all the things you like, the things that comfort you, as well as the worry, the fear, the thought that tomorrow is another day. It means reframing your thinking. Want to change your bubble choice at this point or are you happy with it?

Don't be mistaken – bad habits are hard to break all at once. Change is a gradual process and no doubt you'll have many attempts before you feel that things seem right. Making the change though means being realistic about what you actually can achieve. Learn to say 'Yes' and 'No' to what's manageable. Remember – 'little steps, small rewards, big results' – and you'll get there.

Reframing your procrastination.

Procrastination is full of negative language. Language affects your thoughts. Thoughts affect your feelings. Feelings affect your motivation, your doing ... and so you're blocked and stuck. Why not write yourself a letter about all of this? Tell yourself exactly how things have been and, if you had one wish, how you would like to change it all. Now read the letter aloud. How does it feel having written something? Can you scale it?

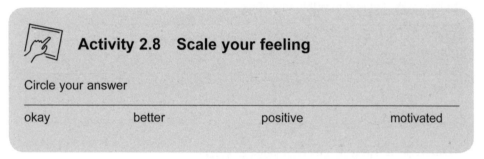

Activity 2.8   Scale your feeling

Circle your answer

| okay | better | positive | motivated |

Trying to reframe your procrastination habit but don't exactly know how? Why not try the 'Move From, Move To' strategy to help you override a negative thought with a positive one.

Move from   Move to

I can't handle this situation   I can do this

I'm afraid of failing   If I try then surely I'll do well

What's the point of even trying?   I need to try so I can achieve my goal

Ever tried writing a positive thought on a card, keeping it in your pocket and pulling it out when the going gets tough? That strategy can help to reframe your thoughts and enable you to move from the negative to the positive. Or, if you prefer, capture your thoughts in a

Activity 2.9   Traffic light, all systems go!

Still putting things off? Why not try the traffic light system to look at the bigger picture, then prioritise and categorise things. Check your progress and what still needs to be done. Revisit your learning style (Chapter 1) or the assignment planning stage (Chapters 4 to 6), if need be. Stop putting off the reframing process – do it now! Oh, and remember to pencil in some 'me' time, so you get the balance of study and play in your student life.

Red tasks – attend to that day

Do	Done
Do	Done

Amber tasks – attend to within the week

Do	Done
Do	Done

Green tasks – can wait until next week or longer

Do	Done
Do	Done

sketch and pin it on the noticeboard where you study. And so, with that, you reframe the belief you have in your own ability.

Prioritised and categorised – change should seem more possible now!

Step 5: Reviewing the change

Change is a good thing; it's positive. It's a process that questions your fears, your self-belief, your motivation, your commitment. You'll never really understand how much change has taken place or how much

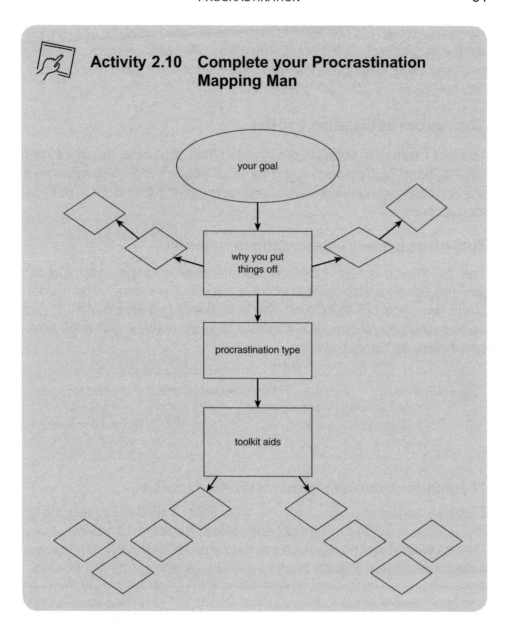

Activity 2.10   Complete your Procrastination Mapping Man

you've progressed until you've looked at two points: where you've come from and where you're at now.

Draw a picture of your successes; place them inside the Mapping Man. At the same time, list the hiccups you've experienced along the way and show how you've overcome these or learned from them. The Mapping Man can provide a picture of how you use the Steps to arrive at this point. State your goal and add the main ingredients to this changing pattern – the tools and the strategies, the manageable and the achievable, and the people who support and sustain your change.

Have you made real change? Is there some loose change, or have you short-changed yourself? Don't worry, just get back on track and keep peddling away. Change is possible. Face your fears, take responsibility and feel proud of your achievements!

Your procrastination toolkit

The procrastination toolkit is designed to help you break the mould and get into gear. There's something for all of you in the toolkit, regardless of your preferred learning style or where you might feel stuck in the five-step process.

The visual learner's procrastination toolkit

This will let you create a picture, visual image or diagram so you can see the connections in how you do things. That way, you'll under-stand why you put things off and eventually get stuck. With better understanding, you might be able to face your fears and take some small steps to move forward.

- Bubbl.us
- Coloured stickers
- Dabbleboard
- Inspiration
- Little Book of Procrastination
- Mapping Man
- Mind Genius
- MyWebspiration
- Progress chart
- Storyboarding

The auditory learner's procrastination toolkit

This has something for everyone who finds it easier to hear things first, jot them down or highlight with colour so the information sticks. There's even music in the toolkit to help you relax while working away, a digital recorder to listen back to your ideas and people to chat to.

- Background, relaxation music
- Coloured stickers
- Digital recorder
- Notebook
- Peer support
- Personal tutor
- Progress diary
- Scribbling doodle pad
- Student Adviser
- Timetable
- Traffic Light System
- Wall planner

The tactile learner's procrastination toolkit

Enjoy making a model or creating a poster with colour and shapes? If this method of working makes your learning and understanding easier, then this toolkit is just for you. Things like a stress ball and worry stone will help your concentration and keep you focused when studying.

• Academic poster	• iTunesU podcasts	• Stress management
• Activity book	• Mindfulness exercises	• Subject-related online
• Arts and crafts toolbox	• Mini reflective journal	activities
• Background, relaxation music	• Progress chart	• Wobble board
• Cardboard	• Stress ball	• Worry stone

Look back to your learning style (Chapter 1), match up your toolkit and dip in and out of them at any time. Perhaps using a combination of tools from each toolkit will help you work through your blocks better and feel that you're progressing. Once you find the tools that work best for you, stick with them. Don't try to change; otherwise, you might find you become stuck again!

Lightning ideas

- Understand the task and what you need to do
- Look at the bigger picture and see the small parts that make this up
- Prioritise and organise each part, and create your routine
- Set realistic deadlines for the bigger picture and for each chunk
- Tackle the small parts in small manageable chunks – use a timer
- Tackle the part you find easiest first – no need to work through things systematically
- Make the task interesting
- Write your Task for Today
- Record your progress by scoring off your deadlines task by task
- Learn to say 'no' so you can tackle your task without any distractions
- Take regular breaks to relax and unwind
- Reward yourself once each task is completed
- Be confident about what you've done by writing something about your achievement each day
- Change your thinking pattern to change your procrastination pattern
- When you think of something, do it; don't just think about it
- Be persistent in your efforts

Little steps, small rewards, big results

 Please go to the Companion Website for this book www.sagepub.co.uk/gribben to access downloadable resources, all the activities featured here and a podcast for this chapter.

3 Note-taking

This chapter deals with the before, during and after processes involved in dealing with lecture material. It presents strategies to improve your note-taking skills, and helps you connect old knowledge with new so you can make the most of your lectures.

| Lectures | Note Nuggets – what, why, how | Connecting before lectures |

| Connecting after lectures | Your note-taking toolkit | Lightning ideas |

Lectures

Oh, how good it would be to have good lecture notes! That would make me feel so much better about myself. I'd feel I was getting the point of the lecture and have something good to go on when working on assignments and revising for exams.

I'm always working out different ways to take notes but nothing seems to work.

My lecturer talks too fast and I can't keep up. I always leave with half-done, scribbly notes and feeling hopelessly lost.

Listening, looking, remembering and writing – forget it; I'm not a juggler!

I can't remember everything the lecturer says.

How often have we sat in lectures and switched off because we've lost track? Missed the key points and so left with incomplete notes and a bundle of frustration? Even sat in a lecture with cramping hands because we're trying to write down every single word that comes out of the lecturer's mouth? Sound familiar? Then let's change the way you think about lectures.

Remember, there's no right or wrong way to take notes. As long as it works for you and your learning style, then it's right for you! Of course, taking notes is made easier if your lecturer has good delivery skills. How much more interesting things become! A good lecturer will:

- distribute lecture notes (in an accessible format) before each lecture
- begin the lecture by giving a general overview of the subject
- outline the main ideas to be covered
- present headings or key points
- ask questions
- provide evidence from recent research
- provide references
- connect to the previous lecture, if part of a series
- inform you about the next lecture in the series
- most of all, engage his or her audience!

Take note though – you're not meant to remember and write down every single thing the lecturer says; it's impossible and certainly not expected. What's expected is that you learn the difference between what's important and what's not, so you can become an effective note-taker. So why take notes? How useful are they?

Simple really – as much as you might want to just sit and listen to what's being said, you can't avoid taking notes in lectures. Whatever you do, don't switch off because you've been given a handout! Make the most of your lecture: take notes, stay focused on what's said and get involved in any discussion. Of course, notes have an added value. They're your revision tool, your subject encyclopaedia, your learning map.

Note Nuggets – what, why, how

When it comes to taking notes, different courses require different note-taking styles. Art and Design, for example, uses more graphical storyboarding than, say, History, where flow charts detailing historical sequences are useful. Regardless of the style, do your notes work for you? If not, then it's time to re-think your note-taking style.

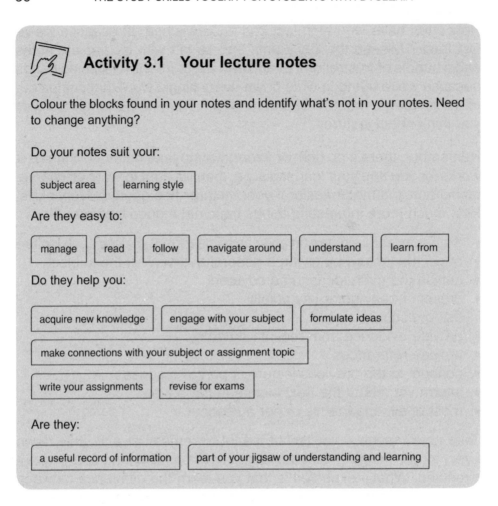

Activity 3.1   Your lecture notes

Colour the blocks found in your notes and identify what's not in your notes. Need to change anything?

Do your notes suit your:

| subject area | | learning style |

Are they easy to:

| manage | read | follow | navigate around | understand | learn from |

Do they help you:

| acquire new knowledge | engage with your subject | formulate ideas |

| make connections with your subject or assignment topic |

| write your assignments | revise for exams |

Are they:

| a useful record of information | part of your jigsaw of understanding and learning |

Table 3.1   Note Nuggets – what, why and how

What's note taking?	It's an information-gathering process; a building block that helps to give you comprehensive knowledge of your subject area.
What are notes?	They're key points of your lecture or resource material; the bare bones of the topic, your knowledge bank and revision resource.
Why take notes?	Taking notes is an important part of your studying and learning experience; it links this new knowledge to what you already know to build up a picture of your subject area.
How do I...?	Practise! Match your learning style with your note-taking style; experiment and find what works for you.
How useful are they?	Very! This goes for your learning, writing and revising.

By taking notes you're:

- being introduced to a new topic
- engaging with the subject

- highlighting key points relating to the topic
- formulating ideas
- recording your own thought processes
- recording important points for future reference
- managing your information
- focusing on key issues as a starting point for learning
- building up your knowledge bank
- gaining some insight into the standards expected of you and into the exam content
- linking information with other material you've resourced for assignments or exams
- revising for exams, even at this early stage
- setting the stage for exam success.

I don't know how to take notes; I've never done that before. I'm a rookie!

OK – you're a new student learning about a new topic and everything's all so new. Learning new skills like note-taking takes time; we've all been there. So while experimenting with your note-taking layout and approach to find what works best for you, take a step back and think – when taking a telephone message, do you jot down:

- every single word that's said?
- a shorthand version of key points only?

Find key points only work? Then why not use the same system for taking lecture notes. Take a lead from the lecturer's handouts and focus in on the key points. If it's mentioned there then it's worth noting! Everything you need to learn about the topic isn't going to be mentioned in the lecture anyway – only the main issues. You'll build a picture of the topic when you research, read, think, make notes and revise. So don't waste time trying to write down every single thing. Keep things simple; don't make your notes look like the latest novel. Be selective! Decide what's important and what's padding; check the handout. Map out the key points before the lecture; keep this in front of you during it. Oh, and do yourself a favour, don't nurture information overload by annotating more than you actually need to know or will use.

Summarising

Want to develop an understanding of the topic? Need a clear outline of issues being discussed? Then summarise your notes by:

- looking for the key points relating to individual themes
- discarding irrelevant information
- writing information in your own words
- putting them in paragraphs, bullet points, lists, flow charts, mind maps, storyboards.

Speed note-taking

Want to speed up your note-taking? Then why not create your own abbreviation system, one that means something to you, that's user-friendly and easily recognisable after the lectures. Oh, and make it easier on yourself by using the same abbreviation system in all note-taking situations. As well as becoming fast and efficient, you'll also have user-friendly notes around revision time or when working on an assignment.

Table 3.2   Useful abbreviations

A	abr.	abridged
	app.	appendix
C	c.	circa
	C.	century
	cf.	see; refer to
	ch(s).	chapter(s)
	cld	could
	%	care of
	col(s).	column(s)
	concl.	conclusion
D	dev.	development
E	ed(s).	editor(s)
	edn	edition
	educ.	education
	e.g.	for example
	esp.	especially
	et al.	and others (four authors or more)
	et seq.	and the following (referring to page numbers)
	etc.	and so on; and the rest
F	f.	following (ff: plural)
	fig(s).	figure(s)
	fn.	footnote

G	govt	government
I	i.e.	that is
	impt.	important
	incl.	including
	inf.	below (referring to a section further on)
	info.	information
	intro.	introduction
J	jn.	journal
K	k	thousand
	kg	kilogram
	km	kilometre
L	loc. cit.	at the place quoted
	LTM	long term memory
M	ms(s).	manuscript(s)
	mgt	management
N	NB	please note – important
	nec.	necessary
	no(s).	number(s)
O	op. cit.	the work quoted
P	p.	page (pp. = pages)
	para(s).	paragraph(s)
	pop.	population
	pt	point
R	ref.	reference
S	sect.	section
	shld	should
	sic.	informs that exact words are used
	STM	short term memory
	supra	above
	tog.	together
T	trans.	translator; translated by
	viz.	in other words
V	vol.	volume
	w/o	without
W	wld	would

Table 3.3   Texting language examples

c	see		2	to, too, two
u	you		2day	today
ur	your		2moro	tomorrow
btw	by the way		2nite	tonight
atm	at the moment		4	for
fyi	for your information		4got	forgot

Why not create your own note-taking text abbreviations using Webopedia?

Table 3.4   Symbols and their meaning

&	and	∴	therefore
+	plus; in addition to	£	pound sign
>	greater or more than	$	dollar sign
<	smaller or less than	€	euro sign
=	equals	√	square root
@	at; at the cost of	≡	identical to
%	percentage	≤	less than or equal to
*	asterisk	≥	greater than or equal to

Table 3.5   Grammatical symbols, their meaning and their use

Symbol	Meaning	Indicates
!	exclamation mark	strong feeling
.	full stop	end of a sentence
,	comma	a pause
?	question mark	end of a question
" "	inverted commas	direct speech
' '	quotation marks	emphasis or when quoting
'	apostrophe	possession
( )	parenthesis	additional information
[ ]	square brackets	a clarifying word or phrase in a quotation
…	ellipses	that words are missing but the sentence continues
:	colon	additional information after an independent clause
;	semi-colon	a longer break in sentences
–	dash	a break in thought or that a list follows
_	underscore	an emphasis of something
/	forward slash	a break in lines; a space
•	bullet point	a list of information

 Activity 3.2   Test your note-taking skills

1. Read the passage, highlight key points and bullet them.
2. Write a summary of the passage's main message.
3. Stuck? Then chat to a friend about the main points, the message and ask for feedback.

Most people are aware that as students they are expected to make notes of some sort. They are aware that these notes would form some sort of record of their studies, and that they will need this record to help them remember key points. Maybe they intend to use the information in the notes in their assignments and exams …

However, we have noticed a change in student behaviour over the last few years. When we started teaching, students tended to take down too much information. They would write page after page of notes that tried to capture everything a lecturer was saying, or everything that was in the book. But recently we have seen students who sit through lectures making no notes at all. We have also seen those who think they can get a degree without doing any reading, let alone making notes of their reading. Now none of these strategies is going to prove particularly useful to you as a student:

- Making too many notes is too passive: you do not need to take down pages and pages of information when in lectures or when reading. But you do need to take down new information, preferably just in key words or phrases, to seed further thought.
- Making no notes – from lectures or reading – means that you are not really engaging with your learning at all. You might be there in body, but you have left your mind at the door (Burns and Sinfield, 2008, p.165).

Succeeded here and want more practice? Work with a friend, make a note of the main points in a television documentary, compare your notes and give each other feedback. Remember, practice makes perfect; as long as notes are workable for you then that's perfect.

Using your Note Nugget example

- brainstorm and generate new ideas
- clearly communicate thoughts or ideas

- connect new ideas with old ones
- enhance your knowledge

INSPIRE YOUR LEARNING
WITH INSPIRATION
- CONCEPT MAPPING
- GRAPHIC ORGANISER
- MIND MAPPING
- WEBBING
- OUTLINE
30.11.11
SOFTWARE

Connecting before lectures

Even before your first lecture, you'll know what topic will be covered. You might even have access to notes on Moodle or some other online source. So why not make the lecture more meaningful and interesting by reading up on this beforehand? Use your Note Nuggets to highlight key points, important dates, names, concepts, theories or practices, and make a note of any questions you'd like to ask.

First lecture over? Then start preparing for the next. Read your own notes, the lecturer's notes and any additional materials. Anything basically that lets you connect old knowledge with the new from lectures; these are connections that help your understanding, particularly if your lectures are part of a series. Remember, the ideas you take into the lecture are just as important as the information you take from it. Both contribute to your learning process and help develop your thinking skills, making connections to other information you acquire from other sources.

Connecting after lectures

What you put in is what you get out – with a little extra knowledge and experience. So don't lose it, use it. Part of refining your note-taking skills is what you do with your notes after the lecture. It's not enough to sit in a lecture, listen to what's being said, take a few notes and

 Activity 3.3   Connections

Trace a line between the 'what to do' and 'what it gives you'. See Appendix 3 on the Companion Website for answers.

What to do	What it gives you
always read your notes immediately after the lecture	facilitates both a global understanding of the topic and deeper learning
type up or rewrite notes	promotes deeper thinking and learning and gives ideas for future note-taking techniques
compare notes with others	helps your reading and understanding, and is another way of revising. Also lets you complete details

(Continued)

(Continued)	
What to do	What it gives you
annotate any thoughts, ideas and questions	aids your understanding of the lecture and is the start of your revision
link new information to what you already know	lets you fill in any gaps, giving a fuller set of notes
talk lectures over with others	makes it easier to retrieve information
file notes systematically as you make them	works as a point of reference for future research and discussion

then stick them in a file to be looked at later. No, work with them – read, sort, rewrite and work out a visual recall system that supports your learning style, promotes active learning and understanding.

Re-working your notes after the lecture also helps identify your lecturer's presentation patterns, your annotation patterns, and helps prepare you for the next lecture. Connecting with your notes also provides a basis for developing meaningful notes for writing assignments or exam revision.

Your note-taking toolkit

Taking notes is a vital part of your learning process. Good notes are key building blocks in your house of knowledge but they're not something you produce just like that. Effective note-taking takes a lot of practice and working out of the tools and strategies that work best for you.

The visual learner's note-taking toolkit

Do you learn best using images such as mindmaps, seeing patterns in information? Then picture your notes, picture your learning!

- Bubbl.us
- Exploratree
- Flow charts
- Highlighters
- Inspiration
- Mind Manager
- Mindmeister
- Note Nuggets
- Sticky text highlighter strips
- Storyboarding
- Study Buddy
- Topicscape
- W.Cube-It

The auditory learner's note-taking toolkit

Prefer to have copies of notes so you can listen and make sense of the lecture? Why not support your learning experience by recording what's being said? Fill in the gaps by reading the notes and listen to the lecture later. The auditory toolkit will support you.

- Audio notetaker
- Digital recorder
- Evernote
- iPhone

- Lecturer
- Livescribe Echo Pen
- Notebook

- Note-taking peer group
- ritePen
- Subject dividers

The tactile learner's note-taking toolkit

If you learn best by 'practice makes perfect' methods, then the tools in this toolkit will support your 'do it, learn it' note-taking skills.

- Academic poster
- Arts and crafts toolbox
- Background, relaxation music
- Coloured labels
- Coloured notepads

- Floorsize Mapping Man
- Post-It question marks
- Sbuddy
- Scribbling pad

- Shaped stickies
- Study group
- Webopedia
- Wisemapping

☀ Lightning ideas

Before the lecture:

- Read up on lecture topic
- Is this lecture a new topic?
- Is it part of a lecture series?
- What's important to learn about this topic?
- How can I connect this new information to my previous knowledge?
- What questions or comments do I have?

- Check your recording device functions before each lecture
- Use a different coloured notebook or folder for each subject, each semester
- Organise your folders with coloured subject dividers and label – lecture, citations, formulae, concepts
- Write the lecturer's name, and title and date of the lecture on each page

During the lecture – choose what works for you:

- Split your notebook page between notes and comments
- Write on one side of the page only; use adjacent page for additional comments
- Write in the middle of the page and add mind map comments
- Leave a margin at the side for additional information or references

---

- Write on every second line so you can add examples or key points
- Personalise your writing shortcuts – abbreviations, symbols, colours
- Use Note Nuggets and build your wall of knowledge
- Maintain a consistent note-taking system

- Keep together issues that belong together
- Cross-refer and link up points
- Make important points look important!
- Discard the padding

- Use mind maps or flow charts
- Use bullet or number points
- Use headings and sub-headings
- Write key words and ideas, not full sentences

- Use a different coloured pen when writing quotations
- Use a different coloured pen for references
- Record any relevant questions or points raised by fellow students
- Create a record of your thinking around the topic – comments, reactions, views, questions – highlight and explore later

---

- Hear better, be distracted less – sit at the front of the class
- Share note-taking responsibilities with a friend
- Revise lecture notes immediately after the actual lecture
- Doodle on a doodle pad, not in your notebook

Hear it, note it, see it, learn it – recall it!

 Please go to the Companion Website for this book www.sagepub.co.uk/gribben to access downloadable resources, all the activities featured here and a podcast for this chapter.

4 Understanding Your Assignment

This chapter helps you to understand your assignment so your response is considered, balanced and answers the question set. It looks at the key asking words in the task set, what they mean and what you need to do next. If you've a clear understanding of what you need to do, you'll be sure to do well.

| Assignments | Understanding your assignment question |

| Understanding your assignment criteria | Understanding what you need to do next |

| Your assignment toolkit | Lightning ideas |

Assignments

Words, words, words – what do they all mean? Ever lost valuable marks because you missed the point of the question? Didn't quite understand what it all meant? Words, hmm …

Every assignment comes with a point to it; it requires a specific approach and it demands a considered response, but at one time or another we've all missed the point and wondered why.

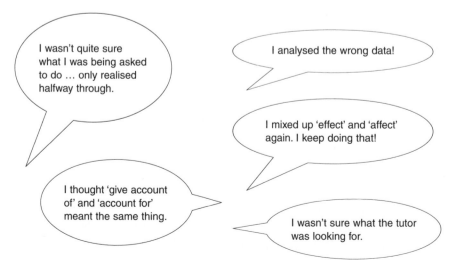

I wasn't quite sure what I was being asked to do … only realised halfway through.

I analysed the wrong data!

I mixed up 'effect' and 'affect' again. I keep doing that!

I thought 'give account of' and 'account for' meant the same thing.

I wasn't sure what the tutor was looking for.

And what did that lead to? .... Panic once we'd realised we'd spent a great deal of time answering the wrong thing. Let's face it, it's simply a question wanting an answer but is it really that simple? How do we know what the lecturers are looking for? Do we always understand the concepts? How do we know what we need to do to answer the question?

There are three points really:

1 Understand the question
2 Understand the criteria – what the examiners are looking for
3 Understand what you need to do next.

Understanding your assignment question

Every assignment question has different layers.

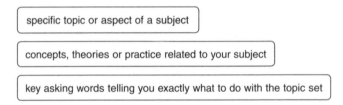

Key asking words – what are they exactly? Well, they're instruction words, words that tell us to do something such as compare, discuss, evaluate, judge – the 'what we must do' to answer the question. Take compare, for example – aren't you doing that all the time anyway?

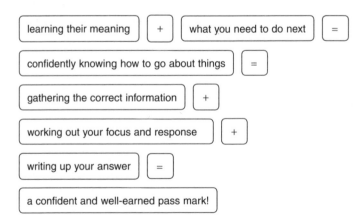

Comparing prices, products, service, efficiency? Even in exams, aren't you comparing the questions to see which seems easiest to answer first? Remember, the meaning of the key asking words and their instructions don't change regardless of what you're being asked to do.

So, take time at the start of your studies to learn the technique and save time, stress or even failure in the long run. Where to start? First, let's test your knowledge.

Activity 4.1   Question – from word to meaning

Trace a line to link the key asking word with its correct meaning:

Key asking word	Meaning
account for	to think carefully about
consider	to state the exact meaning of
define	to give a general plan of
describe	to examine and evaluate something
evaluate	to give a detailed account of
outline	to give an explanation of
review	to show the development or progress of … from beginning to end
trace	to judge the value of

Wondering how well you've done? Then check Appendix 4 on the Companion Website (Key Asking Words Dictionary) for the answers.

If you can, make use of your first assignment or class test, look at past exam papers and past assignment questions from your course, and make a note of the most frequently used verbs and concepts. Break things down and read so you understand:

1 the meaning of every word in the question
2 the words in context so you can understand what the question is actually asking

Make things easy for yourself – refer to your Key Asking Words Dictionary. Still not clear? Then check with your tutor or study buddy so things are clear before you decide which question you want to answer. Oh, and before deciding, don't be fooled into thinking that shorter questions are easier and longer ones are harder – that's not the case.

Shorter questions mean you need to create some thematic structure in your answer, while longer questions often give you step-by-step processes to follow, often indicating what they want to see in your discussion. Don't forget though – short or long, make it easy on yourself and choose an assignment topic that you're really interested in and know most about; not something that, at first glance, looks easy to answer.

Being interested in what you're writing about should help keep you motivated. Your enthusiasm will make your examiner enthusiastic about reading your work, and that's always a good thing! On a more practical note, writing about something you're interested in may save time researching something you don't really know much about.

Activity 4.2   Question – breaking down the bits to understand the whole

Highlight the key asking words in these questions; colour or circle them, then box the concepts, theories, technical terminology and bullet point the topic's focus, e.g. a biomedical approach.

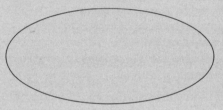

-
-
-

1 Define the terms 'computer-based learning' and 'face-to-face educational support'. Consider their strengths and limitations with respect to contemporary educational thought.

2 Children with secure attachment experiences will have positive emotional connections towards others as an adult. Discuss.

3 Describe the biomedical approach to healthcare and outline the differences between that and one alternative healthcare approach.

4 Public behaviour can be adequately changed using legislation. Judge the value of attitude change initiatives and their actual impact in society.

5 Client A: 'I believe that the Contractor is fully responsible for handing over a quality building.'
   Client B: 'The quality of the finished building is the responsibility of the Client. After all, their expectations can only be met if they fully establish their requirements at the beginning.'
   Critically examine Client A and Client B statements in the context of the contractual provisions under SBC/Q/Scot Standard Form of Building Contract to ensure 'Quality' and present your findings as a discussion paper.

6 Use your interpretation of the poem, or an extract of it, to produce a set design. Your design must have at least one scene change in it, which will involve altering some part of the physical set (25m wide x 18m deep x 20m high). To add another dimension to your set and to bring it to life, you are also to consider a piece of music that could accompany your interpretation.

Activity 4.3   The Meaning Wheel

Subject-related concepts, theories or practices are central to any assignment question. Knowing what they mean, where or who they came from, and how they fit in your question are key to your ability to competently answer your assignment. So, to help you grasp and understand your subject-related terminology, make a note of the ones that frequently pop up in your course discussions and assignments.

Concept, theory, practice - what it means, where or who it came from and how to use it in your assignment.

The Meaning Wheel sample

Concept = working memory

Where or who it came from = psychologists, Alan Baddeley and Graham Hitch

Theory = three components: central executive, phonological loop, visuo-spatial sketchpad

What it means = actively hold information in your mind for immediate linguistic or perceptual processing

So how do you use it in your assignment? Check your key asking word, detail the focus, define the theory and Baddeley and Hitch (1974) viewpoint, examine findings from literature to support or refute the statement, and present a logical argument.

Now complete your own assignment Meaning Wheels.

Starting to become familiar with the processes involved in breaking down the bits so you understand the whole? Want to practise some more so you become more proficient in analysing and understanding? Then work with your study buddy: make up your own questions, practise highlighting the key asking words, work out what the question is asking and test how well you understand what you need to do, to accurately answer the question.

So many diverse written assignments, all looking for different things

Portfolio	Essay	Report	Article	Blog	Poster

Discussion paper	Design brief	SWOT analysis	Digital story

Online magazine	Reflective journal	Literature review

Précis	PowerPoint	Case study

Problem-solving task

Documentary film script

Storyboard	Lab manual	News article

Accounts analysis	Short question paper	Dissertation project

Brochure design	Conference plan	Design toolkit	Data analysis

Log book	Diary	Advert	Letter	Mindmap	Newsreel

Understanding your assignment criteria

Depending on your subject area and year of study, you could be asked to do all of the above assignments or even some of them at different points in your course. So knowing the format, word limit, weightings and what's expected of you should help inform your planning, organisation and the approach you take when researching information, making notes and writing your assignment. Regardless of the assessment format, the general assessment criteria examiners tend to look for are:

your knowledge of a specific topic and its connection to a wider topic and subject	your understanding of the specific theories, concepts, graphical images and practice related to your subject
your critical thinking and ability to argue and debate your viewpoint with supporting evidence from literature	your ability to give a clear, considered, balanced and well-structured academic response

More specifically, for example, the assessment criteria for Activity 4.2, Portfolio question 5 are:

1 Demonstration of applied knowledge and interpretation of procedural issues
2 Consideration of both the Traditional procurement and the Design and Build Procurement contexts
3 Correctness of relationship drawn
4 Essay writing skills
5 References to relevant Case Law

Table 4.1   Styles and what this means

Styles	What this means
Subjective	writing from your own personal perspective; presenting your own views, opinions or experiences
Objective	writing as an outsider with no personal experience
Qualitative	presenting an interpretative account of people's experiences in an objective manner
Quantitative	presenting information that can be numerically measured
Analytical	presenting a detailed, critical examination of a subject
Argumentative	presenting and supporting your viewpoint with evidence, while considering opposing viewpoints at the same time
Comparative	presenting similarities and (or) differences between different viewpoints or evidence
Descriptive	presenting details in a narrative manner
Discursive	presenting clear points of discussion
Evaluative	presenting information that gives a balanced view of a topic, e.g. both differences and similarities, and that reaches an informed conclusion from the evidence presented
Factual	presenting the facts only of the topic
Reflective	examining a situation against existing practices and (or) theories

Some example questions for these styles might be:

1 The human rights of offenders are considered more than those of their victims. Discuss. (Argumentative)

2 Compare and contrast European Special Educational Needs legislation with that of Britain. (Comparative)
3 Describe the differences you have experienced between the theory and practice of infection control in clinical practice. Consider
   how these differences affect your own practice. (Reflective)

In some practitioner-based courses, you'll have formative and summative assignment styles (with often the former leading on to the
latter). Different formative assignments require a different approach
but, as an example, you might be asked to:

Define the term holistic and consider how the claim to holistic practice might influence the
emerging relationship between complementary and general medical practitioners.

- Formative – forms an outline of the chosen assignment topic,
  shows how it will develop and any references you'll use

The formative measures your process of learning a particular topic;
any gaps found in your formative plan will be identified by your tutor.
So use the comments to help improve your summative assignment.
Don't lose valuable marks by launching into writing the summative
before your formative has been approved.

- Summative – presentation of the actual assignment

Now it's time to work on your summative assignment. Want to stay focused
on the summative writing? Then use your formative plan as a guide.

Understanding what you need to do next

You've understood the question and what the examiners are looking
for, now it's time to figure out what you need to do next to answer that
question confidently and correctly. Check Appendix 4 on the companion website for that step. Having already linked the key asking word
with its meaning (Activity 4.1), you now need to link it with the 'what
you need to do next' option in Activity 4.4.

To see how well you've done, check Appendix 4 on the Companion
Website for the answers.

Grasped how to go about things? Want to get started now? Then
brainstorm! Alone or with your study buddy or group, the first step
in any assignment is to get your initial thoughts down on paper:

Activity 4.4 From asking word to what you need to do

Trace a line to link the word with what you need to do next.

Key asking word	What you need to do next
account for	find and consider the evidence, the advantages and disadvantages, and reach a conclusion
consider	find the main characteristics or features
define	find the beginning and end of ... and the stages in between these
describe	find the important details, leave out the minor details, and show how they are interrelated
evaluate	find reasons for
outline	find evidence to support your point of view
review	look for the key features
trace	find evidence to support the advantages and disadvantages

one word, one idea and let it develop from there. So let's brainstorm! Don't be surprised, though, if you don't use every single brainstorming idea in your assignment; you most likely won't! Some may be more relevant than others, some not as important as you first thought.

So, jotted and noted, what you do next becomes smoother. Clearly knowing what you know and what you need to know, you:

- don't waste time reading irrelevant texts
- can easily sort out the important from the irrelevant
- can distinguish the main ideas from the related ones
- can clearly map out where you're taking the discussion.

Your assignment toolkit

Understanding your assignment demands different activities to support your learning style. Different people need different building blocks to figure out what's required in the assignment set. So dip in and out of different toolkits; find the things that work for you so you become skilled in understanding any assignment. This also makes it easier to decide which assignment question to answer.

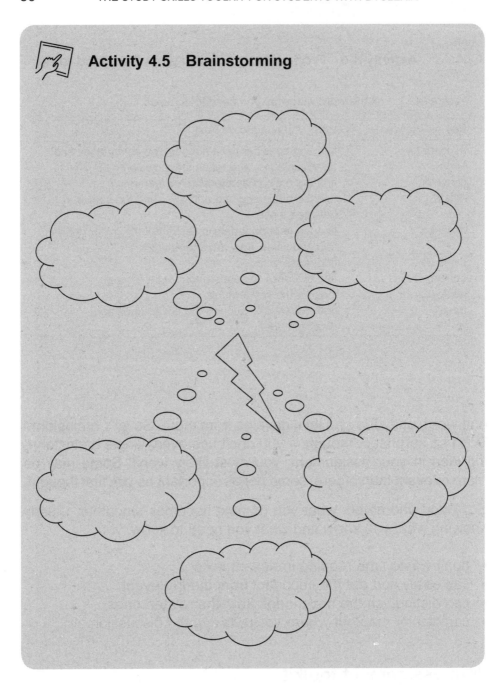

Activity 4.5   Brainstorming

The visual learner's assignment toolkit

Do patterns and connections make sense to you? Does seeing things in bits and then as part of a whole picture support your learning processes? Then sharpen your skills by connecting with the visual toolkit.

- Academic poster
- Coloured stickers
- Exploratree
- Key asking words dictionary
- Mapping Man
- Mindview
- Notebook
- Peer support
- Personal tutor
- Sticky text highlighter strips
- Traffic Light System
- Topicscape

The auditory learner's assignment toolkit

Sometimes hearing the question can make it clearer – words make sense, you understand the concepts and then you get the point! So dip into the auditory toolkit and refine your comprehension skills.

- Background, relaxation music
- Coloured stickers
- Digital recorder
- Index cards
- Key asking words dictionary
- Notebook
- Personal tutor
- Project book
- Smartsheet
- Study Buddy

The tactile learner's assignment toolkit

Want to get to the point where you instinctively understand your assignment? Refining your skills by practising and doing things hands-on; seeing the building blocks and the bigger picture of your assignment? Then get to grips with learning tools in your tactile toolkit.

- Academic poster
- Background, relaxation music
- Coloured stickers
- Dabbleboard
- Mapping Man
- Personal tutor
- Speech bubbles – shapes
- Shaped Post-It stickies
- Study group
- Study skills workshops
- Traffic Light System

 # Lightning ideas

- Read the entire question through twice at least
- Question the question – what are you asking me to do? What do I need to find out?
- Highlight the key asking words – circle or colour
- Highlight concepts, theories, practices – box them
- Break long questions down into bullet-point sections

- Write asking words, meaning and what to do next on shaped stickies
- Copy the asking words, meaning and what to do next three times at least
- Place the different-shaped stickies on your study board
- Create a shaped mind map of asking words, meaning and what to do next
- Record asking word, meaning and what to do next, then listen to it

---

- Write the question in your own words
- Read the question aloud
- Record the original question and your interpretation of it, then listen to it
- Check you've understood your assignment with your tutor or study buddy

---

- Write your assignment question on one side of an index card, your interpretation of it on the other and check them in spare moments anytime, anywhere (or store them electronically)
- Keep focused on the assignment task – make a question card and always have this in front of you while researching, reading, note-taking and writing your answer

---

- Use your key asking words dictionary (See Appendix 4 on companion website)
- Practise past papers, past assignment tasks and podcast exercises
- Work in a study group or with a study buddy
- Learn your subject-related concepts, theories and practices

---

- Make a note of the diverse assignment tasks on your course
- Check your tutor's expectations
- Check the assignment criteria

- Learn from previous assignments – make a note of ways to improve your understanding and your overall response
- Don't alter the meaning of the question to suit your knowledge
- Don't write everything you know about the topic, only what the question is asking

Understand the bits to understand the whole

Please go to the Companion Website for this book www.sagepub.co.uk/gribben to access downloadable resources, all the activities featured here and a podcast for this chapter.

5 Gathering Information

This chapter looks at the processes involved in gathering information from the library and online resources. It takes you through the searching, finding and using stages of effectively sourcing what you need for your assignments, and tells you how to avoid plagiarism.

| Searching | Finding | Using |

| Your gathering information toolkit | Lightning ideas |

Searching

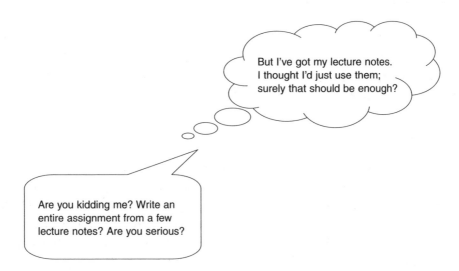

How many of us started out thinking that's how it all worked? Then realisation dawned – we needed to learn to use the library ... What!? Library!? That place full of books and print!? That place where the letter–number system is so complicated we never seem to find what we're looking for and so ... exit the library from our student life?

Is that such a wise thing? Of course, there will always be students who'll never use the library, but how successful are they really as students? It's true, you'll already know something about your assignment topic from lectures and notes, but you'll always need to know more. So ask yourself – am I here to scrape a pass or am I here to understand my subject so that eventually I can enter the working world as a confident, knowledgeable professional? What's it to be?

It's true, libraries can be difficult to use but they're not impossible to manage. Even accessing online resources can sometimes be hard but still manageable. So instead of dreading the searching and the surfing in the hope you get it right, why not join forces with fellow students, share responsibilities and make this part of your assignment interesting, exciting, even intriguing (see Chapter 1). Don't forget, some like online surfing, while others prefer hard-copy searching. So play to your strengths and see what all this information gives you. Oh, and brainstorm – what do you need to know to make your search run smoother? Job shared! Does searching and surfing seem too much like hard work now or too scary a thought? Right, let's make a start!

By taking time at the start of your course to learn your library's systems and procedures, and online and search engine processes, you'll save time and energy later on. Know your subject section, bookmark your favourites and learn how to search effectively.

Learn how to search

Different assignments require different types of searches. So identify the scope and type of information you need. Is it books, journals, newspapers, online, audio-visual? Is it historical or current? Is it scientific, legal, governmental, general theory, practitioner-related? Is it key to your discussion or for background information? Generally, you'll have a reading list but if you don't then search using key concepts, subjects, topics, words to find what you need. Remember, save your search for future reference!

- catalogue – simple search, advanced search, electronic searches, search engines
- catalogue system:

†‡†‡ Activity 5.1　Library treasure hunt

From opening times to inter-library loan procedures, make learning about your library fun by allocating tasks in your group. Record key information in your W.Cube-It (Chapter 1): one section – one issue.

What's your library's ...

opening hours	
catalogue referencing system	
search engine system	
limit on the number of borrowing items	
photocopying regulations	
individual or group study room booking system	

Find out ...

How long can I borrow:	How do I borrow:
• standard loan books • short loan books • reserve section books • inter-library loans	• inter-library loans • inter-campus library loans • audio-visual materials • electronic or digital copies
How do I:	How do I use:
• reserve books • renew books • get extended loan periods as a reasonable adjustment • resource accessible materials	• reference sections • journals • special collections • digital resources • maps

Now hunt for these:

1　medical dictionary
2　legislation on the use of mobile phones while driving
3　a book from your course you need to borrow through an inter-library loan
4　two articles on virtual e-learning environments
5　self-issue machines (and find out how they work)
6　the title of Diana Ridley's academic book.

In your W.Cube-It, jot down where you found them and the sources you used to search. Now write a few sentences on how this activity made you feel or helped you. Share it with your group.

- o books: numbers = subject; letters = beginning of author's surname
- o journals: numbers = subject; letters = beginning of journal title

- journals – name, year of publication, volume number, article title, abstract
- your subject section:

  - o standard loan, short loan, reserve, reference, special collections
  - o media collections, electronic information, digital resources

- national library catalogue system.

Your online search

Finding information online has become the norm for many students. Many courses encourage the use of online reading materials. Searching locally or remotely, at home or worldwide, accessing online materials has its advantages and disadvantages.

Table 5.1 Advantages and disadvantages of online material

Advantages	You can: • access the most up-to-date, 'hot off the press' research • access when and where it suits you • change the font size and background colour so you can read and print articles to suit your needs • have control over the material and search engines you use • store search engines in your bookmark favourites • see an overview of what's available on your topic • evaluate whether a text is relevant to your topic • gather, store, reference and share information using online referencing tools • access information at the same time as others without being restricted by a loan period encountered in borrowing hard-copy texts.
Disadvantages	You can: • easily cut and paste, and so are more open to plagiarise • restrict your reading to online materials only and miss an important hard-copy text • inaccurately cite a reference.

Want to optimise your bookmarked search and access academic works worldwide? Then add Google Scholar, Google Books and iTunes-U to your course's recommended search engines and databases. If your university subscribes to electronic resources then you're sure to find what you need. If not, then try an inter-library loan. Not quite enough? Then widen your search using online search engines.

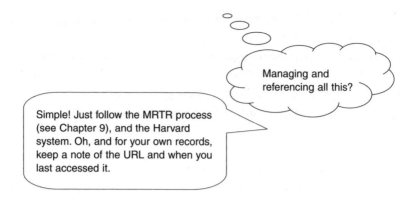

Managing and referencing all this?

Simple! Just follow the MRTR process (see Chapter 9), and the Harvard system. Oh, and for your own records, keep a note of the URL and when you last accessed it.

A referencing example

Leeds Metropolitan University: Skills for Learning (2009) Quote, Unquote: A guide to Harvard referencing [Internet], Leeds: Leeds Metropolitan University. Available from http://skillsforlearning.leeds met.ac.uk/Quote_Unquote.pdf [Accessed 1 March 2011].

Finding

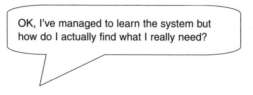

OK, I've managed to learn the system but how do I actually find what I really need?

Table 5.2   Scanning

What you're doing	• looking for a word or a phrase related to your topic; rapidly searching through library catalogues, search engines and printed information • scanning over then skimming to make sure it's what you need.
How you do it	• search the library catalogues to find materials related to your assignment topic • scan the contents and index pages looking for relevant chapters and themes • place Study Buddies bookmarks in the relevant pages • cross-reference, making a note of all the pages that contain the same themes – easier to locate for more detailed, close reading • list pages and their related topics • use a fresh page for each topic and the YOP code for your references (YOP code: Yellow = book; Orange = journal; Purple = online resources).

To help you get a kick-start on personalising your surfing and searching system, why not read over Chapter 1 and take it from there. Want to keep track of your searches and what you've found so you can share it with your group? Then use the online Zotero or EndNote. First though, you'll need to learn how to scan and skim for information. Not sure how? Confused? Need some practice?

Table 5.3   Skimming

What you're doing	• quickly casting your eye over key words and phrases related to the topic, generally missing out the small in-between words • getting a general sense of the issue being discussed so you'll know it's exactly what you need.

How you do it	• record the topics and references you need for your assignment
	• use Study Buddies bookmarks to identify information in texts
	• read information relating to one single topic at a time, and skim read, searching for phrases or concepts that relate to the topic
	• use shaped stickies to make a note of these
	• to discuss different viewpoints in your assignment, then use
	
	    o Mapping Man One – the 'for' viewpoints
	    o Mapping Man Two – the 'against' viewpoints.

Let your Mapping Man organise your thoughts, group information and references, and help you decide what to use and what to discard.

Using

How many of us thought we were great students because we were sitting in a library? How many of us were actually studying? Were we using the information we'd just found or simply trying to look good? Finding information is one thing but knowing how to use it effectively is another. So how do you use what you read so you can confidently produce work worthy of your knowledge? Learn your detailed and close reading processes, (see Tables 5.4 and 5.5), use your MRTR process (Chapter 9) and make use of text-to-speech software to aid your understanding.

Avoiding plagiarism

Avoiding plagiarism isn't easy and is something every student grapples with but it's something you need to be aware of, from gathering information through to writing up.

Table 5.4   Detailed reading

What you're doing	• reading each word at normal speed
	• understanding and considering what your reading is all about; its main message
	• not making notes at this stage – simply reading, considering and evaluating its relevance for your assignment.
How you do it	• work through the topics one at a time to consider the relevance of it for your assignment
	• make a fresh Mapping Man and colour-code the various topics using a different shape of the man for each one
	• colour-code the references and match them against the shaped and coloured topic
	Now using index cards:
	• write your reason for using each particular reference – where does it fit in your discussion?
	• put the coloured shape of the topic it belongs to at the top of the card
	• put all the information that belongs together in a plastic wallet in your assignment folder.

Table 5.5   Close reading

What you're doing	Involves all of the above – scanning, skimming, detailed reading plus reading more closely, so you can take notes for your assignment.
How you do it	All of the above strategies plus:
	• develop a Mapping Man or list to make notes of the information you intend to use
	• practise summarising what you've read
	• add your own thoughts and ideas, and chunk information according to its topic.
	Create a Mapping Man picture of your discussion to make writing up easier:
	• use a large Mapping Man for a bigger picture of the assignment topic
	• use a smaller Mapping Man for the arguments, thoughts and ideas associated with the bigger picture
	• use the same shapes and colours for the same viewpoints
	• record all references accurately to avoid plagiarism
	• remember that you don't have to agree with everything you read. If you disagree then make a note of it and say why
	• be confident about your agreements and disagreements, and what you're writing.

So always:

- check and follow your university's guidelines on plagiarism to avoid its consequences
- follow the MRTR process
- run your work through Turnitin.

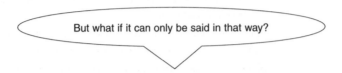

But what if it can only be said in that way?

We've all come across views and ideas where we feel there's simply no other or better way to say things. It can only be said in that way – succinctly and to the point. If that's the case then don't waste time trying to rewrite the un-rewritable; simply acknowledge the source and reference it accurately.

But what if I like the way the author says it?

Equally, don't become complacent and fill your work with endless quotes that fail to demonstrate your understanding. Just because you like the way something is written doesn't mean to say it's stating exactly what you're trying to say. After all, you'll have read it, thought about it, agreed or disagreed, and evaluated its place in your discussion, so you'll need to demonstrate your understanding in the quality of your academic writing and debate. Show you know your stuff!

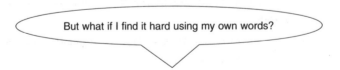

But what if I find it hard using my own words?

Of course, it's hard using your own words, even learning to write academically; it's not something you can do overnight. It all takes practice and confidence! The more you practise, the more confident you'll become. Watch your own writing style develop. How often have we all looked back at assignments and said 'Who on earth wrote that? Was that really me?' That's a sign of development!

> But what if I don't have time to rewrite things in my own words?

Don't make lack of time your excuse. Manage your time and you manage your writing. It's all too easy to fall into the 'no time – panic – copy and paste' trap of plagiarism, collusion or thesaurus overload, but what have you really learned?

Table 5.6   Plagiarism, collusion and thesaurus overload

Plagiarism	copying exactly what the author has written without acknowledging it
Collusion	cutting and pasting content, words or ideas from another student's work to create your response
Thesaurus overload	randomly replacing several key words from others' work to make it appear different and often without knowing exactly what they mean

Remember, your tutor will soon learn your writing style so don't take cutting and pasting short cuts that have consequences. To avoid the obvious:

1 Accurately reference all sources and use Turnitin.
2 Discuss ideas with others but don't show them your work.
3 Use word prediction tools and listen to the options so you understand the meaning.

ŤŤŤŤ Activity 5.2   Summarise and paraphrase

Work with a friend to test your summarising and paraphrasing skills:

- summarise this chapter
- paraphrase one section each.

> But how do I know when to stop gathering information?

If you feel your assignment question can be adequately answered, then trust your instinct and know that you've gathered enough information. Remember, you can't put everything you read into your assignment, even if it seems remotely relevant. So stop reading and making notes, and confidently start writing.

Your gathering information toolkit

Gathering information can be made easy by searching, finding and using tools in this toolkit.

The visual learner's gathering information toolkit

From sourcing to using what you've gathered, these tools should give you the picture memory you need to recall the processes involved when dealing with information.

- Endnote
- Evernote
- Highlighters

- Mapping Man
- Sticky text highlighter strips
- Turnitin

- W.Cube-It
- YOP code
- Zotero

The auditory learner's gathering information toolkit

Feel you'll refine your surfing and searching skills by hearing what's involved? Then this toolkit is ideal for you.

- Android
- ClaroRead
- Dragon
- Flashcards
- Highlighters

- Index cards
- Librarian
- Livescribe Echo Pen
- Quote, Unquote pdf
- Read & Write

- Sticky notes
- Sticky text highlighter strips
- Student mentor
- Study Buddy

The tactile learner's gathering information toolkit

See it, hear it, do it …it sticks! If this is how you learn best, then working with this toolkit will support your learning style.

• Academic poster	• Highlighters	• Library group
• Floorsize Mapping Man	• Index cards	• Smartsheet
• Google Scholar, Google Books	• iQ Mobile Search	• Sticky notes

 ## Lightning ideas

Practise:

- oral summaries using a recording device

- oral summaries with a friend

- written summaries; have a friend read and verify these

- summarising the assignment question

- summarising main points of text

- paraphrasing text

- secure your photocopied pages

- accurately reference the source at the top of each photocopied or printed page

- don't highlight information in library books or journals

- record references accurately

- accurately attribute citations to the exact source

- where possible, rewrite quotes in your own words

- be confident about writing in your own words

- bookmark search engines and references as favourites

- use Zotero, Evernote or Endnote

- use Turnitin

- form a library group – share information

Learn to search, search to learn

Please go to the Companion Website for this book www.sagepub.co.uk/gribben to access downloadable resources, all the activities featured here and a podcast for this chapter.

6 Thinking Critically

This chapter helps you to understand what's meant by critical thinking, and to put it into practice in your assignments.

| Thinking | Becoming a critical thinker | Developing your critical thinking skills |

| Putting your thinking into writing | Your critical thinking toolkit | Lightning ideas |

Thinking

We all think, every day, every minute; from passing thoughts to more considered ones, it's part and parcel of who we are and what we do. Sometimes our thinking can change our views and influence our decisions. It can enhance our understanding, develop our knowledge or awareness of something, and even make us hungry to learn more.

That all seems understandable, but how many of us were confused the first time we read 'critically evaluate', 'critically examine' in an assignment? And so we were introduced to critical thinking …

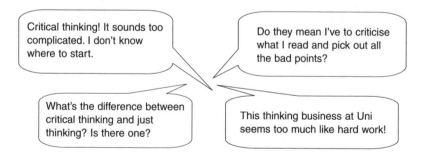

Once you know the difference between critical thinking and the more everyday thinking, and understand the processes, you'll quickly develop confidence and skills in your studies. So what's the difference and what's expected when I'm asked to think critically?

The Oxford Dictionary defines 'thinking' as: 'the process of considering or reasoning about something' (http://oxforddictionaries.com/definition/thinking). It defines 'critical' as: 'involving the objective analysis and evaluation of an issue in order to form a judgement' (http://oxford dictionaries.com/definition/critical).

Now apply that to your thinking at university. This means that when you're asked to critically examine someone else's written work, you need to be objective; to remove the emotion from what you read – even if you're passionate about the topic. You need to look carefully at what he or she says and make a judgement about it. Do you believe

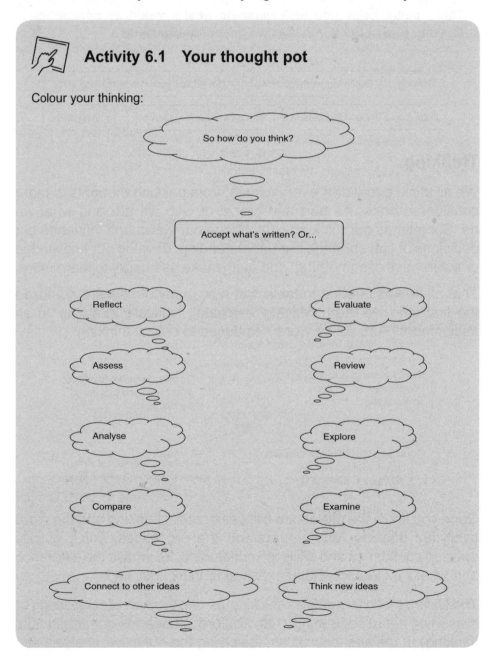

Activity 6.1   Your thought pot

Colour your thinking:

So how do you think?

Accept what's written? Or...

Reflect

Evaluate

Assess

Review

Analyse

Explore

Compare

Examine

Connect to other ideas

Think new ideas

it? Are you convinced? If not, why not? Need some practice to help you understand the difference?

Now think of a situation in everyday life where you've used one of these thinking skills. Do you read, question, think new ideas and develop your own views? Do you sometimes change your mind and make new decisions on your thinking? Now work with some friends; put an everyday situation in a thought pot, compare and discuss the ideas. Learned anything new about the way you think?

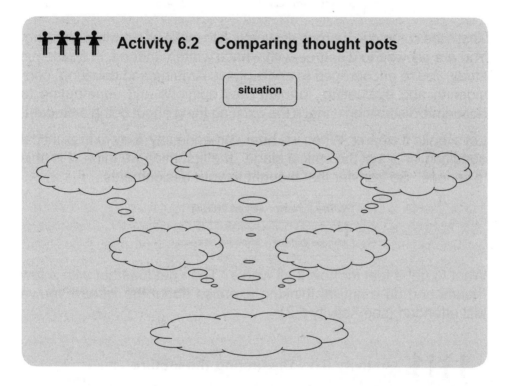

Activity 6.2   Comparing thought pots

situation

Why not repeat that exercise relating it to your assignment. What's your assignment thought pot? Starting to make more sense now?

Critical thinking may be intellectually demanding but it's manageable and achievable. Now you've understood a little more about how you think in everyday life and what's required when doing assignments, let's see what it takes to become a critical thinker.

Becoming a critical thinker

Thinking critically at university doesn't mean you're expected to become a great philosopher in life or a great inventor. Of course, you may go on to be that but while you're studying, it means you can think about an argument, make assumptions, consider diverse viewpoints and their supporting evidence, formulate opinions, develop arguments, and draw conclusions. To be able to do all that, it's important to have an open and enquiring mind that's hungry to learn.

Don't assume that:

because it's printed you need to agree with it	because your lecturer says it you need to accept it
you can't argue against it and give your own opinion	you can't have a view and debate it

That's the commonest wrong assumption to make about critical thinking. You *are* allowed to disagree with what's written. Indeed, in academic study, you're encouraged to challenge it. Arguing and debating, considering and evaluating, forming new opinions and contributing to academic discussion – that's the exciting thing about being a student.

Let's make it clearer. When we hear someone say 'they're in a critical condition' or 'it's at the critical stage', the first thing we think of is 'this is serious'. So transfer that thought to your assignments.

critical thinking = serious thinking

serious thinking = following processes

Want to get a feel for how it all works? Then get together with a few friends and do a critical thinking exercise about the lecture you've just attended (see Activity 6.3).

†††† Activity 6.3   Dissecting the lecture

Use your Note Nuggets (Chapter 3) to focus your thinking. Discuss:

- What was the lecture all about?
- What's the main message you came away with?
- Why does the lecturer want you to accept this main message?
- How did he convey his message:
  - present information?
  - present an argument with supporting evidence?
- What was good about what he said?
- Was there anything not so good about what he said?
- Did he encourage you to think more about what was said?
- Do you agree or disagree with what was said – why?
- Are there any connections with what you've already learned?

With that done, ask yourself – do you want to examine a bit more so you can learn some more? Yes? Then let's look at the skills you'll need to become a good critical thinker:

- think clearly and objectively
- evaluate the author's viewpoint
- analyse the author's argument
- compare and contrast different viewpoints
- identify the points missing in arguments
- identify the strengths and weaknesses in arguments
- evaluate the evidence against the author's statement
- check the accuracy and validity of evidence and data presented
- be dissatisfied until all the evidence is gathered and considered
- develop a more accurate understanding of an issue
- consider the bigger picture and any implications
- make connections between old and new knowledge.

With some practice, you'll develop these skills, become confident in your ability to be critical, and look at the evidence objectively. Applying these skills should improve the quality of your thinking when doing assignments.

Developing your critical thinking skills

Now you've some insight into what makes a good critical thinker, why not evaluate your own strengths and weaknesses in how you currently think. This should help you start to develop your critical thinking skills so that your learning and your writing become more considered, balanced and more interesting.

So that's the critical thinking bit but how do you translate this into writing in your assignments?

Putting your thinking into writing

Critical thinking makes you more confident in your learning, more independent in your ability to question and argue, and more considered in your writing process. So demonstrate that confidence in how you present your academic discussion.

Sort the information – remember what belongs together, goes together.

1 Create separate information lists or mind maps.
2 List viewpoints in a logical sequence.
3 Match for and against accurately referenced evidence to viewpoints.

Activity 6.4   Core and fingertips critical thinking skills

Picture your critical thinking skills and then place the core strengths you've mastered inside the Mapping Man's body. Then, in the arms and legs, place what's at your fingertips – those things you find hard and still have to work on so they too become part of your core thinking skills.

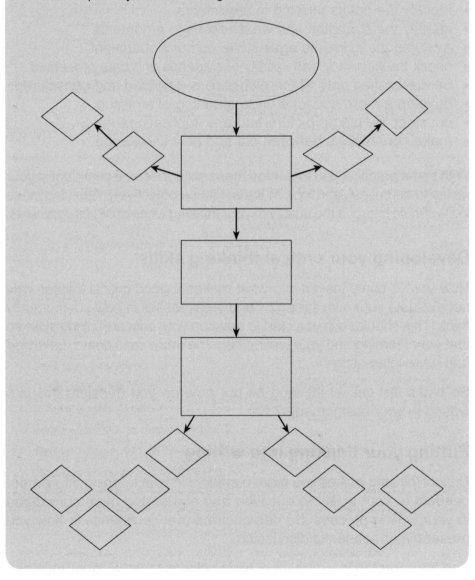

Present the information – maintain a clear and logical line of argument or reasoning while keeping focused on the big questions in critical thinking.

Activity 6.5   Critical thinking wall

Use your Note Nuggets and note-taking strategies (Chapter 3) to build a personal critical thinking wall and see your skills develop:

- main message
- key points
- your initial thoughts
- what you agree with and why
- what you don't agree with and why
- additional evidence you need to support your views
- sufficient, current and up-to-date evidence to support the main argument
- flaws, gaps or bias in the author's argument
- missing links between the main argument and evidence presented
- additional information that connects new knowledge with old
- a clearly structured and focused line of reasoning.

And with that done, what's the clear conclusion? How solid is your wall?

Introduction

1 Say what you're discussing and why
2 Say how you'll approach this – sequence
3 Say what you hope to discover

Main body of discussion

1 Present author's viewpoints and supporting evidence
2 Present arguments against this viewpoint with supporting evidence
3 Present flaws, gaps or bias in author's viewpoint and evidence that identifies these
4 Present your viewpoint with supporting evidence
5 Cross-reference viewpoints and evidence to support your line of reasoning, and make logical connections between these

---

Conclusion

1 Summarise your main arguments
2 State how these relate back to the question and main argument
3 Justify your position – has your view changed? If so, how and why?
4 Identify any implications for the wider research environment or disciplines

Your critical thinking toolkit

Knowing the difference between how you think on the surface and how you critically think can make all the difference to your success as a student. This toolkit can help identify where you're at and support where you're going in developing your critical thinking skills.

The visual learner's critical thinking toolkit

Do you see and understand things better when you can picture the different bits in your head? Do things make more sense when you use images, shapes, pictures, patterns and you can see how everything connects? Then the visual toolkit will support your critical thinking skills and your learning processes.

- ClaroIdeas
- Coloured stickers
- Dabbleboard
- Exploratree
- Mapping Man
- Mindview
- Notebook
- Note Nuggets
- Shaped stickies
- Sticky text highlighter strips
- Traffic Light System
- Wisemapping

The auditory learner's critical thinking toolkit

Does discussing concepts and theories help you unravel the muddle in your head, clearly think things through and help you see where others' opinions fit with your own viewpoint? Then dip into this toolkit and let hearing information make a difference to how you think and learn.

- Background, relaxation music
- Coloured stickers
- Digital recorder
- Index cards
- MyStudyBar
- Notebook
- Personal tutor
- Read & Write
- Study Buddy

The tactile learner's critical thinking toolkit

Want to feel confident about your thinking skills and expressing your viewpoint? Actively practise your thinking; see it concretely unfold before you? Then get to grips with your tactile toolkit and you get to grips with your critical thinking.

- Academic poster
- Coloured stickers
- iMindMap Mobile Pro
- iTunesU podcasts
- Mapping Man
- Personal tutor
- Shaped Post-It stickies
- Speech bubbles – shapes
- Study group
- Thought pot

Lightning ideas

- Read your information and make notes
- Build your critical thinking wall with Note Nuggets (Chapter 3)
- Separate for and against viewpoints
- Separate for and against evidence
- Identify what's convincing and why
- Identify flaws or gaps in the argument
- Identify hidden assumptions
- List your challenges to the argument, say why plus your supporting evidence
- Discuss with your study buddy or study group
- Do a SWOT exercise – Strengths, Weaknesses, Opportunities, Threats

Learn to think, think to learn

 Please go to the Companion Website for this book www.sagepub.co.uk/gribben to access downloadable resources, all the activities featured here and a podcast for this chapter.

7 Writing Your Assignment

This chapter helps you understand the processes involved in writing your assignment. It deals with practical points such as structure and academic language, and suggests ways of dealing with writer's block, so you can progress from your first draft to the finished product.

Written assignments	Plan time, plan structure	What goes where
Style of language	Dealing with writer's block	The practical and the social
From first to final draft	Your assignment writing toolkit	Lightning ideas

Written assignments

Try as we might, we'll never get away from having to write assignments at university. It's part and parcel of who we are as a student; it's mainly how we're assessed. Short, long, subjective, objective, graphical, scientific – different assignments require different things. Regardless of the style though, all assignments need planning and structure, and to be written in a language that's academically correct and acceptable. You've understood the point of your assignment, you've read, considered and gathered the information you need so writing up should be smooth, but is it always?

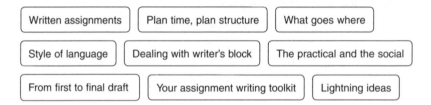

I always struggle to pull it all together. There's so much, it sometimes feels too much.

But, if you plan your time and your structure, it'll seem more manageable.

Plan time, plan structure

Planning is easy but sticking to it is harder. So when you plan, consider the connections in reverse:

- submission to assignment start date
- writing assignment to planning structure to reading material to assignment task
- conclusion to introduction

and consider the contingency plan in case things go wrong.

Activity 7.1 Reversals – note it!

You've been given the assignment, now what's the submission date? Note it! How many weeks away is that? Note it!

Submission date [   ] Number of weeks [   ]

So, what do you know about your assignment topic; what do you need to know? Note it!

Know	Need to know
!	?
_____	_____
_____	_____
_____	_____

Once you've seen things backwards, now work forwards to your submission date, plan your assignment timeline and pace your writing to meet the deadline.

Weeks 1–3: Start resourcing information, reading and making notes, plan your assignment structure.

Weeks 3–5: Critically think; decide what you'll use in your discussion and what you'll discard.

Weeks 6–8: Write up your assignment.

Remember, if you're using a proofreader, you're unlikely to be the only student they're working with. So plan your time well to include a first draft proofread through to a final one.

Week 6: Produce first draft – submit to proofreader.

Week 7: Produce second draft – check structure and content; use Turnitin.

Week 8: Submit to your proofreader for final proofreading; do your final edit; check references.

Week 9: Submit your assignment.

Revisit Chapter 5 when resourcing information, Chapter 6 when you're evaluating this and Chapter 9 when referencing. With that done, keep track of your progress with the 10-step assignment checklist.

Table 7.1   The 10-step assignment checklist

	Assignment submission date: / /	Deadline date	✓
1	Set up your assignment folder	/ /	
2	Analyse your assignment question	/ /	
3	Resource, read, annotate and sort your notes	/ /	
4	Critically think – keep and discard	/ /	
5	Plan your assignment structure	/ /	
6	Write your first draft	/ /	
7	Write your second draft – use Turnitin	/ /	
8	Do final edit	/ /	
9	Do final referencing check	/ /	
10	Do final proofread	/ /	

What goes where

Assignments don't just write themselves. There's logical structure, sequence and a place for everything. So knowing what goes where makes writing that much easier. In any assignment, there's always an introduction to the subject you're writing about, a discussion around this subject and a conclusion to your discussion. So, assignment written, check your conclusion–introduction reversals.

Activity 7.2 Reversals

Conclusion – what you've done

!

_____

_____

_____

Introduction – what you'll do

?

_____

_____

_____

Don't worry about writing the introduction first. It might be the first thing your tutor reads, but it's almost always the last thing you'll write in your assignment. By all means, write a rough introduction so you've a step-by-step guideline to follow when developing your main discussion. In fact, you'll need that to keep your discussion focused and on track.

| Introduction | 10 per cent of total word count |

what you'll discuss: the assignment question re-written in your own words

how you'll go about this: your approach and assignment structure

your hypothesis: reason for your argument and how you intend to prove your hypothesis is right

how you agree or disagree with the assignment viewpoint | key concepts relating to the topic

key points relating to the topic | an explanation or definition of concepts or points

what you'll discuss and why | what you won't discuss and why

previous relevant research you'll use as evidence | sometimes an interesting, relevant quote

final sentence leading naturally to first in main discussion

While you can use the phrase 'main body of discussion' as a guide-line for yourself, don't make the mistake of writing this as your title heading with no obvious structure to this section. Present the exact topic headings in sections and sub-sections – keep yourself and your reader focused, and show where the discussion is going. Always check with your tutor if the section headings stay in or out of the final version of your assignment. When writing your main discussion, tackle the section you enjoy most, know most about and find easiest to deal with first.

| Main body of discussion | 80 per cent of total word count |

first sentence linking from the last one of the introduction   main thrust of your argument

a following of the outline presented in your introduction

your summarised discussion of the topic in sections and sub-sections

one paragraph = one general idea, its purpose and subject matter summarised

paragraphs relating to your original hypothesis

the body of evidence you discuss, accurately cited and referenced

information to verify your argument: dates, diagrams, statistics, graphs

for-and-against examples, evidence, cases, quotations

what you agree with and why   what you don't agree with and why

The conclusion tends to be written at the same time as the final version of your introduction. It summarises all the points you've discussed, and presents any findings and recommendations for future reference. When writing your conclusion, double-check that all points mentioned are reflected in your introduction as issues you'd intended to discuss. They say much the same but in reverse. The introduction starts out with your question or hypothesis and the conclusion finishes by answering it. Did you do what you intended to do? Have you answered the question?

Remember, don't introduce any new material relevant to your discussion in the conclusion. It will be a spare part that just won't fit.

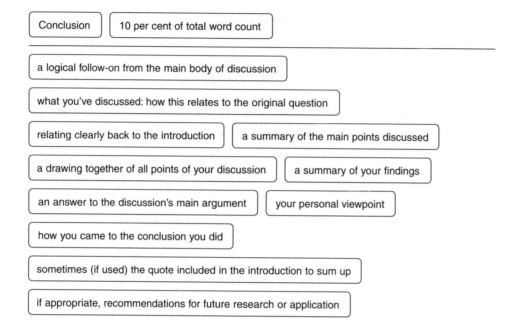

| Conclusion | 10 per cent of total word count |

a logical follow-on from the main body of discussion

what you've discussed: how this relates to the original question

relating clearly back to the introduction | a summary of the main points discussed

a drawing together of all points of your discussion | a summary of your findings

an answer to the discussion's main argument | your personal viewpoint

how you came to the conclusion you did

sometimes (if used) the quote included in the introduction to sum up

if appropriate, recommendations for future research or application

Portfolios

Designers | Teachers | Nurses | Journalists | ...and more!

Different courses require different types of portfolios, so check with your tutor as to the acceptable style and format for your course. Is it all written in the first person ('I') or only part of it? Whatever the course though, a portfolio assignment gives you the opportunity to reflect on your learning and your practice. Writing a portfolio lets you be more active in your learning so you can learn new skills and see your progress as a learner, and a practitioner.

So what's in your portfolio? It's a collection of your work that can contain tasks such as:

Artefacts | Blogs | Essays | Group presentations | Your reflections

Your portfolio is evidence of your achievements and generally presents:

- a brief statement of its purpose in relation to your learning outcomes
- artefacts, if required by your course; say why you specifically included that selection
- evidence of the knowledge and practical skills that support your assignment outcomes
- brief descriptions of that evidence, making connections between course materials and practical experiences
- a reflective section that describes:

  o how the individual pieces of evidence support and meet your learning outcomes
  o what new knowledge and skills you've learned
  o what you feel you've still to master to achieve competency in your subject area.

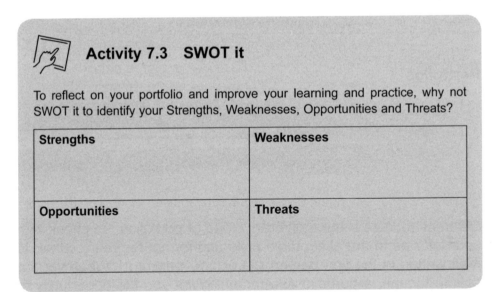

Activity 7.3   SWOT it

To reflect on your portfolio and improve your learning and practice, why not SWOT it to identify your Strengths, Weaknesses, Opportunities and Threats?

Strengths	Weaknesses
Opportunities	Threats

Paragraphs

Paragraphs vary in length; some are short, others slightly longer – generally between four and 12 lines. If shorter than four lines, then your main point hasn't been developed enough and if longer than 12 then you've probably presented more than a single idea, or have included padding. Of course, paragraph lengths depend on what you're discussing but what it's not is one single sentence. It will have:

- one main idea (or points dealing with the same idea)
- sentences that support your main idea
- connecting ideas presented logically and coherently
- enough content to create a unit of meaning in sections or sub-sections
- linking sentences from one paragraph to the next.

Sections

A section deals with information relating to the same issue being discussed. Sometimes sections contain sub-sections (different sub-headings) related to this main issue.

Quotations

We often support our viewpoint by using quotations, so knowing how to manage them is key to developing a robust discussion, and avoiding plagiarism.

Table 7.2   How to use quotations

Do	Don't
• use quotations that support your discussion	• use irrelevant quotations
• use each quotation appropriately and in context	• use a quotation without commenting on it
• record quotations accurately	
• use 'single' quotation marks when quoting directly	• alter the meaning of a quotation to suit your view
• use "double" quotation marks when quoting within a quote	
• if using a long quotation, use three dots (…) (ellipses) to show that some words have been omitted	• use lengthy paragraphs containing irrelevant information as quotations
• if using a part of the original quotation, make sure this makes sense in the context of your own sentence	• use quotations as padding
• if changing words in a quotation to fit the context of your own sentence, put the changed word in brackets [ ]	

Long quotations:

- are generally more than two lines long
- are presented as a separate paragraph
- are indented one inch from the left-hand margin
- don't require the use of quotation marks
- are referenced accurately, citing the page number also.

Below is an indented quotation

> Portfolios are becoming a common form of assessment. It is tempting to accumulate quantity instead of quality, but don't just hurl a load of material in. Tutors will want to see 'evidence' of your achievement in relation to specific learning outcomes. It's sensible to place your evidence (your lesson plan, an extract from a research diary you kept ... an annotated bibliography of reading ...) into appendices and cross-reference these to:
>
> (a) a contents page (closely tied to the specified learning outcomes and/or assessment criteria)
>
> (b) a discussion which highlights what you have learned, and draws attention to the evidence that can be found in your appendices (Sambell, Gibson & Miller, 2010, p.65).

Short quotations:

- are generally up to two lines long
- are presented as a running text within your own sentences
- require the use of quotation marks
- are referenced accurately, citing the page number also.

For example:

In a discussion around different forms of assessment, Sambell, Gibson & Miller (2010, p. 66) advise students on the use of reflective commentaries by stating: 'don't assume that they [lecturers] are asking for personal opinionated writing. Lecturers will be looking for theorised thoughts that show what you have learned'.

Style of language

Wouldn't student life be so much easier if we could write our assignments exactly as we speak? How good would that be – using words we know and like, instead of words we don't always quite understand, and in a way that almost seems foreign to us? Foreign or not, it's a skill we must learn and one that takes time. Learn the skill and master the writing process.

Remember, writing in an academic-style language doesn't mean that you've to write in a way that's complicated, long-winded or difficult to understand. Want to engage your reader? Then write in a brief,

clear, direct, straightforward language style that's readily understood, and remember your academic pointers.

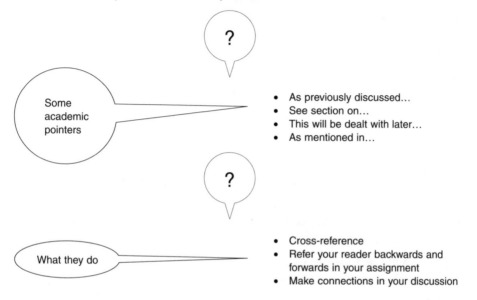

Some academic pointers

- As previously discussed…
- See section on…
- This will be dealt with later…
- As mentioned in…

What they do

- Cross-reference
- Refer your reader backwards and forwards in your assignment
- Make connections in your discussion

Use:

- the third person ('he', 'she', 'it', 'they', 'the writer', 'the author')
- the active voice, e.g. 'students conducted the research'
- the present tense of an author's past reporting, e.g. 'the author suggests'.

Don't use:

- the first person ('I') unless writing a reflective or subjective piece of work, or instructed to do so
- the passive voice, e.g. 'research was conducted by the students'
- contractions of words, e.g. don't, it's, can't
- conversational language, e.g. maybe, really
- figures of speech, e.g. metaphors and hyperboles
- conjunctions at the start of sentences, e.g. and, because, but

- colloquial words and expressions, e.g. sort of, stuff
- two-word verbs when you can use one word, e.g. put off.

When reporting authors' ideas or opinions

Table 7.3   How to reports others' ideas

Use	Rather than
considers or believes	thinks
questions	asks
states or suggests	says
observes	sees
maintains or argues	feels
raises	brings up
appears to be	looks like

 Activity 7.4   How much do you know?

Circle true or false (see Appendix 5 on the Companion Website for answers):

I can add new information in the conclusion	True	False
I can't give my personal viewpoints in my assignments	True	False
I use quotation marks when quoting directly	True	False
I can present longer quotations as separate paragraphs	True	False
Longer quotations are usually more than three lines long	True	False
I can write 'main body of discussion' as my heading	True	False
My main body of discussion is divided into different sections and sub-sections that contain paragraphs	True	False
I can use both numbers and letters at the same time when listing my appendices	True	False
References are works I've cited throughout my discussion	True	False
One sentence can be considered a paragraph	True	False
My main body of discussion contains the main thrust of my arguments, as well as my discussion of the topic	True	False
My conclusion draws together all the main points discussed in my assignment	True	False
Bibliography is everything I've read as background information for my assignment topic	True	False

Dealing with writer's block

Writer's block – that thing we all dread but experience at some time in our student life. Those moments where we stare endlessly at the blank paper or screen waiting for inspiration, thinking we're the only ones who get writer's block. We're not! It's part and parcel of the writing process – books, articles, reports, assignments, exams. Even the most successful writers or most experienced professors get it. No one escapes the dreaded writer's block!

Waiting for inspiration? Don't! It won't come, unless you actively do something about it – talk to others, get their support, doodle your thoughts, record them, shape up your ideas. Know what to do when the block strikes and make sure you don't confuse writer's block with procrastination – they're not the same. What's more, don't make one the excuse for the other. In short:

> writer's block = getting stuck while trying to write and struggling to become unstuck = motivation

> procrastination = putting things off and staying stuck because, well, we all find excuses = lack of motivation

Writer's block comes in many guises and at different stages:

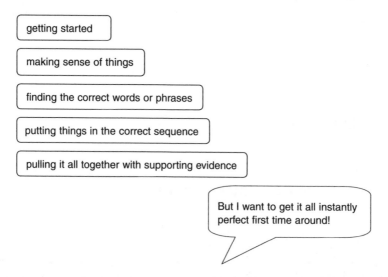

getting started

making sense of things

finding the correct words or phrases

putting things in the correct sequence

pulling it all together with supporting evidence

> But I want to get it all instantly perfect first time around!

Take that view and you're sure to get writer's block – the writing won't happen, the block will. There's no such thing as 'instantly perfect'. It all takes time – thinking, considering, exploring and re-working concepts, refining arguments and viewpoints, and, finally, after numerous drafts, piecing your ideas and thoughts together so that it all makes sense to you and your reader. So, use the strategies that work for you and feel the progress.

The practical and the social

We need practical and social solutions to unblock our writer's block. Using them when we most need to should put us on another track and help re-energise our thinking and our writing. They're not meant as a quick fix – it's great if that happens though! So why not practise some of the solutions in this section and see how they work for you.

Achievable and manageable goals

Make your daily goals realistic, manageable and less overwhelming by creating a work schedule that's realistically productive. Think of the plus in tackling a sub-section and the minus in aiming to complete a full section. So aim small, achieve much!

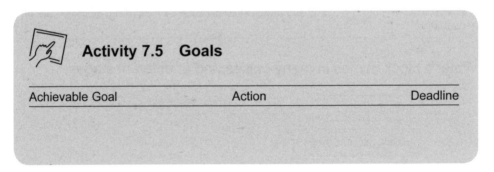

 Activity 7.5   Goals

Achievable Goal	Action	Deadline

Free-thinking writing

Activity 7.6   Think free, write free

Find it hard getting your thoughts on paper? Struggling, feeling blocked? Then do some free thinking writing. Write anything for five minutes – a letter to a friend, a diary entry, a poem about how you're feeling at that moment. Become friends with the paper and the writing, free up your thought processes and unlock your block. How do you feel now? Feel that helped? Can you put words to that?

Brainstorms

Working on the same topic as your friend? Then put your heads together and brainstorm. Chunk your fresh ideas into thought clouds as you're chatting and see what it generates.

Storyboards

Find it easier to tell a story about what you're doing or how you're feeling at the moment? Then picture it and note it, and unravel the muddle in your head.

Topical bookmarks

Create your own topical bookmarks by chunking information that belongs together. Numbering your bookmarks keeps them in sequence when developing your assignment.

Scribbling jigsaws

Things popping into your head but not really making any sense and so you're stuck? Scribbling jigsaws are ideal for noting down your initial thoughts and piecing them all together. Note one idea per card, number or colour them and click one thought into the next to create a jigsaw of each section or sub-section in your assignment. Then:

- add more thoughts and ideas as you go along
- see the sequence of topics in your sub-section
- see the bigger picture for each section.

Blockbuster cards

Unblock your ideas and reduce your stress levels with blockbuster positive thinking cards. Create your own 'use anytime, anywhere' handy-sized pack.

 Activity 7.7   Personalised blockbuster cards

Jot down:

- a positive thinking slogan
- your favourite quote
- a previous challenge or task you handled well
- a positive quality you value in yourself
- a positive quality others value in you
- a stress-busting catchphrase
- a comment about how well you're doing in your studies
- a mini map of your progress
- a mini map of your writing progress
- a note of your goal and reward

Sticky memos

Stickies are great for following up on ideas. Develop ideas from your scribbling jigsaws using the sticky memo. Give your memo a deadline; achieve your goal.

Note Nuggets

Find these worked for you in lectures? Nuggets jotted and noted? Then build a picture of your thoughts by building a wall of nuggets.

Shaping up your ideas

Want to get your ideas down but struggle with lists, mind maps, W.Cube-It, even the Mapping Man? Then shape up your ideas.

Your social keys

Want your writer's block to be short-lived? Then make small changes that physically and emotionally remove you from the situation. Socially re-create yourself and re-create your focus by making small changes.

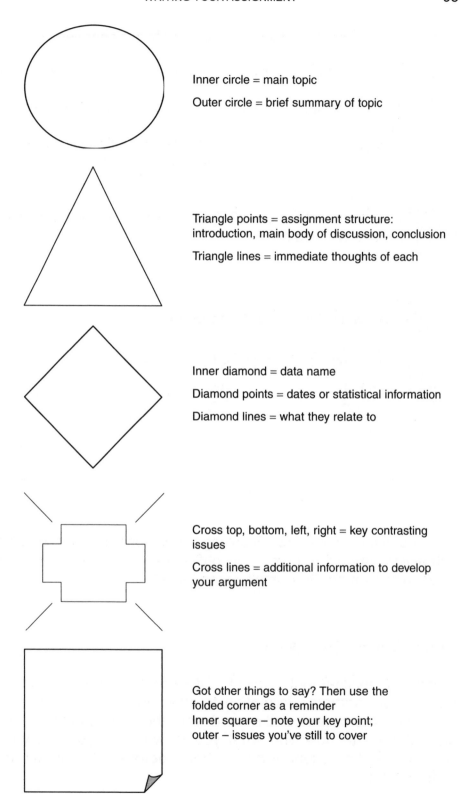

Inner circle = main topic

Outer circle = brief summary of topic

Triangle points = assignment structure: introduction, main body of discussion, conclusion

Triangle lines = immediate thoughts of each

Inner diamond = data name

Diamond points = dates or statistical information

Diamond lines = what they relate to

Cross top, bottom, left, right = key contrasting issues

Cross lines = additional information to develop your argument

Got other things to say? Then use the folded corner as a reminder
Inner square – note your key point; outer – issues you've still to cover

where are you most productive?	channel your energies
your workplace – home, library	physical activities – walk, sports
free up your mind, do some free writing	switch off to switch on later
your landscape – beach, park	pampering activities – a cup of tea, a bubble bath

Still suffering from writer's block? Then explore the problem and not the topic you're working on!

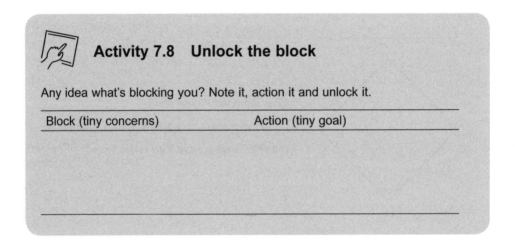

Activity 7.8   Unlock the block

Any idea what's blocking you? Note it, action it and unlock it.

Block (tiny concerns)   Action (tiny goal)

Feel you can manage now? Breaking things down into tiny concerns and actions should give you the confidence you need to move forward and progress. Deal small, progress far.

From first to final draft

Writing an assignment doesn't just happen. It takes shape in stages from sorting information to structuring your discussion. You need time to work and re-work your thoughts and ideas; add and subtract to how and what you've written. Typically, you'll write a first and second draft (or more) before the final edit and final reading.

First draft

The first draft tends to follow the structure you drew up at the planning stage. Once you've read the material and taken notes, you can then formulate your ideas and start writing. During the first draft, you typically cut and paste; add and subtract ideas.

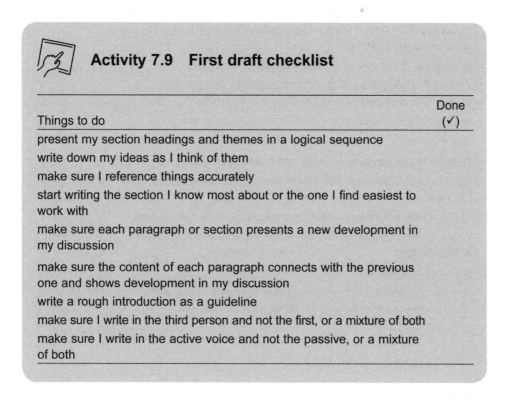

Activity 7.9   First draft checklist

Things to do	Done (✓)
present my section headings and themes in a logical sequence	
write down my ideas as I think of them	
make sure I reference things accurately	
start writing the section I know most about or the one I find easiest to work with	
make sure each paragraph or section presents a new development in my discussion	
make sure the content of each paragraph connects with the previous one and shows development in my discussion	
write a rough introduction as a guideline	
make sure I write in the third person and not the first, or a mixture of both	
make sure I write in the active voice and not the passive, or a mixture of both	

Completed the first draft? Then leave it for a day before reading it again. A fresh pair of eyes and a clearer mind help you work out what's relevant and what's padding. Make changes in the first edit of your work – your second draft.

Second draft (see Activity 7.10)

Now leave your second draft for a day. With fresh eyes and a clearer mind, you'll feel more confident about what stays and what goes. Your final edit is your most ruthless stage – word limit, deadline looming, it's time to be absolutely clear about your discussion and get rid of the padding.

Activity 7.10   Second draft checklist

Things to do	Done (✓)
read over my first draft quietly; does anything jump out that seems out of place or doesn't flow? Highlight this for future reference in a second, closer reading	
re-read my first draft as a close reading	
check the logical sequence of information in sections and sub-sections, and change the order, where necessary	
remove information that's irrelevant, misplaced or is padding	
add information that supports my discussion	
re-write chatty language into formal academic style	
add academic pointers that inform the reader of the sequence of my discussion	
check all my references (including supplementary references)	
check that all my quotations are accurate and correctly acknowledged	
write my conclusion	
re-write my introduction, checking that all points in my main discussion are logically and systematically presented	

Final edit

Activity 7.11   Final edit checklist

Things to do	Done (✓)
check my assignment structure	
check that I've not repeated the same information in several different ways	
make sure my discussion flows logically	

Things to do	Done (✓)
add any academic pointer that I've omitted	
use a thesaurus to give me some alternative words or phrases	
use a spell-checker to correct any errors I've made	
double-check that all my references are accurately recorded	
double-check that all my arguments are supported with relevant evidence	

Final reading

We all do a final reading just to make sure – have we forgotten a reference, does it read OK, are we happy with it? Remember, you can't add anything at this stage. It will be seen as padding, a spare part that doesn't fit, or worse – it could effectively jeopardise what was otherwise a good discussion. So make your final reading just that!

Your assignment writing toolkit

Get to grips with your writing and make how you deal with your assignments smoother by using the tools that match your learning style.

The visual learner's assignment writing toolkit

See the different elements of your assignment develop and take shape by using the visual tools in this toolkit. From initial ideas to final product, this toolkit will support your visual learning style.

- Bubbl.us
- Coloured stickers
- Dabbleboard
- Inspiration
- Mapping Man
- Mind Genius
- MyWebspiration
- Note Nuggets
- Noticeboard
- Personal reference system
- Shaped Post-its
- Sticky text highlighting strips
- Storyboarding
- Topicscape
- Wall planner
- W.Cube-It

The auditory learner's assignment writing toolkit

Never written an academic assignment? Feel you'll learn the processes more easily by being told how to do things? Then dip into this toolkit to sharpen your skills and make writing easier.

- Android
- Background, relaxation music
- ClaroRead
- Digital recorder
- Dragon
- Livescribe Echo Pen
- Mentoring or buddy system
- Mobile A to Z organiser
- Mp3
- MyStudyBar
- Notebook
- Project book
- Read & Write
- ritePen
- Student Adviser
- Study group
- Turnitin

The tactile learner's assignment writing toolkit

Practise and refine your writing skills by using the tools in this toolkit.

- Arts and crafts toolbox
- Assignment timetable
- Background, relaxation music
- Cardboard
- Highlighters
- Hypnotherapy
- Mapping Man
- Mindfulness exercises
- Project book
- Proofreader
- Sticky text highlighter strips
- Stress ball
- Stress management
- Study Buddies bookmarks
- Study skills tutor
- Wobbleboard
- Zotero
- 10-step assignment checklist

 # Lightning ideas

- Plan and write a manageable and achievable timetable
- Use different software for different stages or tasks in your assignment
- Use visual images to capture your ideas
- Jot down your initial ideas in any format, even if you discard some later
- Talk to someone about your assignment's initial ideas and generate more
- Leave time in between the first, second and final reading
- Use your study skills and proofreading support often and effectively
- Don't overload your workspace with too many notes, books, articles when writing: clear workspace = clear mind = clear writing

Plan to write and you're writing to your plan

Please go to the Companion Website for this book www.sagepub.co.uk/gribben to access downloadable resources, all the activities featured here and a podcast for this chapter.

8 Writing Your Dissertation

This chapter looks at the dissertation. Using the Dissertation Diamond, it helps you understand the Deciding, Researching, Writing and Referencing (DRWR) processes involved in producing a gem of a final year paper, from initial conception to finished product.

| Dissertations | D-Deciding | R-Researching | W-Writing |

| R-Referencing | Your dissertation toolkit | Lightning ideas |

Dissertations

Writing a dissertation or working on a practical project for final year honours is now well cemented in university life. Most courses expect students to take on a large piece of work: we've to research it, analyse it, discuss it, report it, make recommendations, even create a product. Finally, we get the chance to work on something we've always been interested in; now is our time to shine! Sounds great!

On a practical level, it helps prepare us for writing large reports in the workplace and gives a good grounding for postgraduate studies. It maybe even kick-starts our career. That sounds great too, but…! How do we crack the dissertation code to produce a gem of a paper?

Apart from our first ever university exam or assignment, the very thought of writing something as huge as a dissertation is probably the scariest ever. Starting out in the first year, the mere thought of writing 1000 words seemed insurmountable, but we did it! Now it's 15,000 words – how do you feel about this right now?

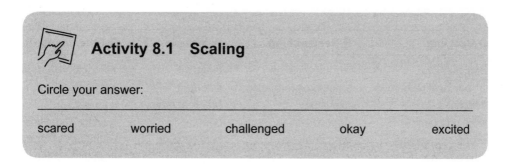

Activity 8.1   Scaling

Circle your answer:

| scared | worried | challenged | okay | excited |

What's your immediate thought?

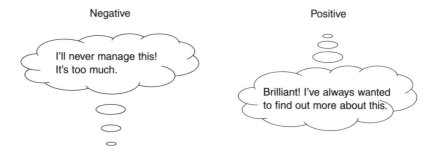

Negative

I'll never manage this! It's too much.

Positive

Brilliant! I've always wanted to find out more about this.

Right, you've got this huge piece of work to do. Surely, getting your Honours is the goal and giving up at the last hurdle isn't an option. So what you need to do is:

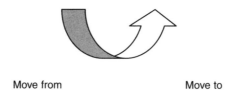

Move from   Move to

Think back to your first ever assignment – how you felt, coped, worked through it all – and how surprised you were when you actually managed to write those 1000 words! What changed? Or what helped you make the change? Does it feel any different this time? Remember, lots of big things are made up of small bits. So take a step back, break it down then work on the bits to achieve the whole. Use your Dissertation Diamond to help you achieve this.

Table 8.1   The DRWR process

D-Deciding	R-Researching	W-Writing	R-Referencing
personal and	literature review	language	abstract
practical resources	sourcing information	first draft	contents
deadlines	pilot study	practical project	sources
topic proposal	data collection	brief	recommendations
scope and sample	data analysis	final write-up	limitations of study
ethics			troubleshooting
methodology			

Dissertation diamonds

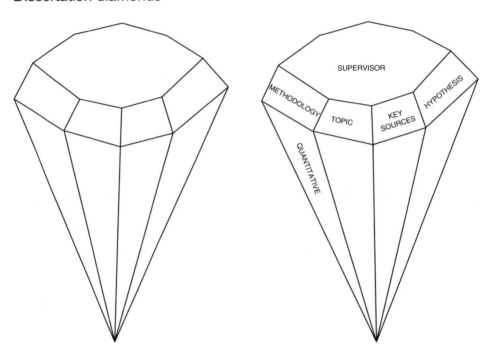

D-Deciding

Personal and practical resources

Working on a lengthy dissertation project can be mentally draining. We can find ourselves becoming de-motivated, unfocused and dis-interested. Then there's the practical stuff that can get in the way. When things happen, what's needed most is some positive input and structured support to help get us back on track. That's always a wel-come thing.

So, key to your support and effectively your success at this stage are:

- your dissertation supervisor
- your study skills tutor
- a proofreader
- practical resources.

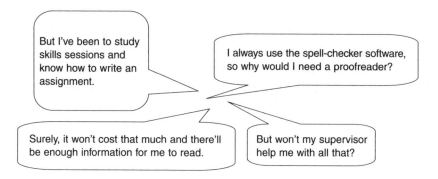

Supervisor

Your supervisor may be able to help with some of it but certainly not all. They'll know your subject so can give valuable guidance on:

- finding a dissertation topic
- formulating your hypothesis
- methodology
- key sources
- proposed dissertation structure.

They can help nurture your ideas, unravel your thoughts when things get muddled and give feedback on draft chapters and your progress. Working independently means they'll guide you, not lead you by the hand every step of the way. So, although they can pick up on errors as they read your chapters, what they can't do is take on the job of proofreading or making sure your dissertation is organised and referenced correctly. That's where the software, study skills tutor and proofreader come in.

Study skills tutor

Of course, you'll know how to write an assignment. Nobody doubts that, but getting some specific guidance when putting together your dissertation project should ensure your study skills are sharpest when you most need them. So take advantage of the support offered by your study skills tutor. As well as mutual support, they can:

- help keep you and your work on track so you meet deadlines
- make sure your chapters are well organised, structured and correctly referenced
- help you make the most of your feedback so your work improves and you feel you're making progress.

Proofreader

Yes, you're at that stage when things need to be refined, double-checked, corrected and accurate. Sure, the specialist software picks up on errors but what about the homophones – those words that sound the same but change the meaning of what you're trying to say? They stick! So don't lose valuable marks because of small inaccuracies or misunderstandings; use a personal proofreader and feel more confident about your final product. Meet up and plan how you'll work together with:

- regular submission dates
- electronic chapter-by-chapter submission
- track change procedures
- final proofing submission 10 days before the assignment deadline.

Want to get the most out of your support? Then remember four key points:

1 You're most likely not the only student your supporters will be working with.
2 Stick to the deadlines, submit chapters regularly and experience your progress.
3 Don't make unrealistic demands and expect your key supporters to drop other commitments just because you've missed a deadline or want something done.
4 If personalities clash, then change who you're working with early on. Don't wait until things become too difficult or muddled.

Practical resources

Dissertations don't write themselves; practical projects don't just appear completed. We've all got to tap into resources of some sort. We've got to source information, respondents, materials, and for some projects that can mean unexpected additional costs. Sometimes participants might need a financial incentive to be part of your study. So source your resources; be clear about what you need and the budget you require. Oh, and when thinking about that, don't make the mistake of choosing a topic with very few literary sources, particularly if researching a theoretical topic.

Activity 8.2 Key costs

literature	
travel involved	
lab materials	
design project	
postage	
materials	
respondents' expenses	
filming	
photography	
photocopying	
printing	
binding	
practical project	
degree show	
design patent	
other	

Remember, this is your life's work at university; want to get it right then get your support right. Choose wisely – plan early!

Deadlines

There's no other way of dealing with deadlines than meeting them. Think of the personal consequences of not managing that. Miss a deadline and you suffer the consequences of the knock-on effect; what you'd planned to do gets pushed further away. Miss another deadline and you're heading for disaster. It's as simple as that – and that's something you can't afford to do on the home-run stage of your degree. So, don't entertain any knock-on effects; note the main deadlines and the small in-between ones, and stick to them.

Remember, your word limit very much determines your chapter deadlines, and your overall timetable. So work backwards to move forwards. Take the final deadline, create a mid-point and divide tasks into blocks of time. Things should seem much more manageable then.

Activity 8.3   Noted deadlines

research proposal   _____
literature review   _____
questionnaire   _____
pilot study   _____
fieldwork   _____
data collection   _____
data analysis   _____
graphical imagery   _____
portfolio   _____
proofreading   _____
final submission   _____

Want deadlines to work for you? Then make a summer start and your final year will start and finish well. Talk to your supervisor, identify your study skills tutor and proofreader, organise your specialist software training and plan ahead. Oh, and touch base often. So, rapport established, topic discussed, mutual expectations clear, deadlines noted, it's now a case of working towards that first deadline – your research proposal.

Topic proposal

Deciding what we want to research is relatively easy. After all, it's almost always something we've always been interested in. We've a hunch (hypothesis) about something and decide to examine it more closely. What's not so easy though is sticking to that decision. We start reading about one thing only to find something else a bit more interesting and then another, and before we know it we've drifted off in a completely different direction. So decision made, make a research question magnet and keep this in front of you at all times – while researching, reading, note-taking, collecting and analysing data, and writing your answer. Be a sticker, not a drifter!

Make your proposal direct and straightforward. Be clear and explicit

Activity 8.4 Sticker or drifter

Make a magnet of your topic so it sticks in your mind as well as on your study board or fridge!

about what you'll do and why, and what you hope to accomplish:

What you'll do = your title, aims (what you intend to do) and objectives (specific questions you hope to answer)

Why = why it's interesting for you, the wider field, gaps in research literature, timely topic

Desired outcomes = practical or theoretical contribution to future research, to the learning or general social environment

Remember to research something that will keep you interested and switched on over a long period of time. Don't make the mistake of choosing a topic because you fancy learning about it or it sounds like a good idea, or which has insufficient reading material. Otherwise, you'll surely become a drifter.

Scope and sample

Scope, sample – what's that exactly?

While the 'where' of your study area is clear from the topic you want to research, working out the 'who, how and what' of your target sample hinges on what you want to find out and from whom:

- What do you want to research?
- Who do you want to question?
- How many people do you want to question?
- What's the best way to find out the information you want?

Ask these questions and frame your study area, target population, sample size and the methods you'll use to find answers to your research question. Don't ask and you could easily be gathering information endlessly from countless people. To meet your deadline, be a sticker – remember the research timescale.

Table 8.2   Scope and sample

Scope	area of study that will help you achieve the purpose of your study, e.g. educational
Sample	number of people who'll answer your specific questions, e.g. honours students in three universities

Your target sample and your respondent sample are always different; response rate is almost never 100% – if by chance it is, then you're more than very lucky.

Table 8.3   Target and respondent sample

Target sample	80	people you want to question
Respondent sample	36	people who answered your questions

So what are the benefits of your respondent sample? What would happen if you asked a different group the same question? Would the data be limited or questions remain unanswered? Remember, you need to report your limited responses as part of your study's limitations.

Ethical considerations

Most universities have procedures for projects requiring ethical considerations. Ask yourself:

- What type of study am I doing?
- Does it have any moral or ethical implications?
- Does it require confidentiality?

If so, then familiarise yourself with the procedures and apply early for any ethical permissions. Confidentiality required? Then sign an agreement with your research subjects and stick to it; respect their position, safeguard your own. Remember, researching sensitive issues requires sensitive questioning, so get approval from your supervisor before asking questions.

Methodology

Qualitative, quantitative – what is it? Which is it?

Oh, how confusing it is the first time we hear the words qualitative and quantitative. Don't quite grasp it? Well, there's 'quality' about the stories in a qualitative study and there's 'quantity' – something we can count – in the quantitative.

| Qualitative | quality – tell it | their feedback experience was positive |
| Quantitative | quantity – count it | 1, 2, 3, 4; about 85 per cent used Turnitin |

The methodology you use depends very much on what you want to find out, and why and how you want to use the information further. If your interest is gathering opinions and views then you'll surely opt for a qualitative study. Need to gather facts and figures for some reason then it's quantitative. Of course, you may also choose to use both methodologies and more than one research tool. Being clear about the what, why and how of your study should make it easier to identify the methodology and the research tools you need to use, to gather the information that best answers your research questions within the data-collection period. Decision made, now justify:

- your chosen method and selected tool
- why you opted to use this one as opposed to another.

Then explain how you'll use these with your identified target sample. See example on page 112.

Worked out the methodology and sorted out your questions, but will it all work? Are your questions clear, to the point and understandable? Will they get an answer or will they end up in your respondent's bin? Want to test it out?

What?

How many honours students use Turnitin and find it effective as a working tool in their dissertation projects?

Why?

The number of honours students plagiarising continues to rise

How?

To inform current practice and develop training and support procedures that engage students in using this tool

Methodology –

Qualitative and Quantitative

Research Tool –

Email questionnaire using open and closed questions

Analysis Tool –

SPSS (Statistical Package for Social Scientists)

How easy did you find using Turnitin? How effective was it in helping you avoid plagiarism?

open question?

- lets you gather more than one piece of information, and can lead to even more information being provided
- respondents answer in their own words

Did you use Turnitin for:

- entire dissertation?
- more than half?
- more than two chapters?
- literature review only?
- other _____?

closed question?

- provides specific, pre-defined answers
- respondents generally give one answer only

Most dissertations contain a pilot study where you can test the feasibility of your study's procedures. Although smaller-scale than the full study, your pilot is vital in:

Do:

provide clear instructions for respondents

use simple, clear, straightforward language

use sensitive language if researching sensitive issues

keep questions and questionnaire brief

cover one issue only in one question

include 'don't know' or 'other' options, where appropriate

categorise and logically list questions

Don't:

deviate from the Do list

- testing your study's plan and design to see whether it's workable
- identifying any defects or potential practical problems that may occur in your main study
- helping you improve the logistics – re-shape questions, approaches, sample, procedures, design materials, film setting, data-collection timescale
- contributing to your main study's success.

Two things to remember about your pilot:

1 Report on it when writing up your dissertation, highlighting your findings and any changes you needed to make.
2 Don't ask the same participants to answer questions in your main study.

If it's a practical design project, test out your prototype – its design, efficiency and usability, and report on this and any changes in your main study.

R-Researching

Literature review

It's that part of the dissertation many of us dread. Reading so much information, working out what it all means, what's relevant and what's not, and reporting it in a meaningful way seems too much like hard work. In setting our research focus though, it's a 'must do'!

Reviewing the literature helps you:

- highlight gaps in the research market
- support or negate your hypothesis
- work out your research questions
- understand how you'll analyse your data
- confidently discuss your research.

So make it interesting, informative and, most of all, enjoyable and it will seem less daunting. One issue covered, then write it up and watch your draft chapter develop. Of course, don't just report it, critically think about it and be critical in reporting. Remember, your opinion counts too, as long as you can support it with evidence. If you don't agree with something then say so and, most importantly, say why.

Data collection

The timescale of your study should help determine when or how you collect your data. Never underestimate the time you need for this, particularly if you're transcribing interviews or focus group discussions, or waiting on postal returns. It can often take longer than you initially expected and can sometimes affect your sample size, response rate and the quality of the data you collect, and in effect your hypothesis. So talk to others, draw on their experience, work out your timeline and stick to it. Don't go searching for additional information when time's limited; simply make the most of the data you collect by using the most appropriate analysis tool. Be clear about how you'll analyse the data before you start collecting it.

Example:

Beginning of January	End of January	Mid-February
Send out questionnaires	Chase up completed questionnaires	Data-collection deadline

---

Activity 8.5   Data-collection timeline

Write your timeline

Starting point	Mid-point	End point
task?	task?	task?

Data analysis

You've gathered information and now it's time to make sense of it; what you've found out, questions answered, questions unanswered. Use the Dissertation Diamond to categorise the information gathered. That done, now apply your analysis tool, such as SPSS.

W-Writing

More than ever, writing up is going to prove difficult. With more reviewing than the smaller assignment; more analysing, critical thinking, academic discussion and logical structure, your dissertation demands more focus and discipline to keep going and ultimately complete.

Writing up's the worst!

How often have we heard that? Even said that? Procrastinated yet again? Felt like giving up? Felt wobbly, as if it's not pulling together? The support is on offer so why not make good use of it and get it right. Take advantage too of the information in earlier chapters and revisit the exercises when you feel stuck:

- Chapter 2 for moments of procrastination
- Chapter 6 for thinking critically
- Chapter 7 for planning and writing up.

Don't slip up at this stage! There could be more than just your supervisor reading your work!

Language

Now more than ever, we need to get the language right. It's not just a case of getting our thoughts down on paper, working on different sections, not really bothering too much about our spelling, grammar or academic language because, well, everybody makes mistakes.

Get your language right – use your spell-checker, study skills tutor, proofreader and check out Chapter 7. Learn:

- what and what not to say
- how to write academic pointers
- how to write in the third person, present tense of an author's past reporting.

Practical project

Not all dissertations are purely theoretical; some are creative and contain practical elements – photography, product design, graphic design, film. If this is your project, storyboard it, record the process in your journal brief, develop your prototype, animation, film or photographic collection. Oh, and, if necessary, test things out in a pilot study. Make time for the practical project while writing the dissertation.

R-Referencing

Abstract

Some do, some don't – but if your dissertation requires an abstract, make your summary clear, concise, understandable and interesting. Engage your reader in less than 100 words detailing what you researched and what you found out.

Contents

Isn't it helpful to see what's in your dissertation? Want to encourage people to read your interesting work? Then follow the contents section in the referencing chapter. Of course, this is your dissertation – a much larger piece of work – so you'll probably write your contents page twice:

1 In the planning stage as a guideline.
2 When you revise it for your final presentation.

Sources

Referencing our work can be a nightmare. We read information to broaden our background knowledge and other sources to include in our research discussion. Know when, where and how to use these

(Chapter 9). Follow the system, get your proofreader to double-check things and gain those valuable marks.

Recommendations

Not all dissertations contain recommendations; they're not always necessary. If you've got some and want your research to make a difference, then be clear about the what, why and how of your recommendations, categorise and note them – the practical, theoretical or points for consideration in future studies.

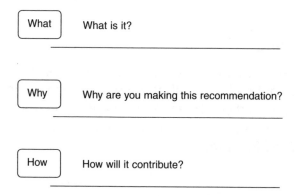

Limitations of study

'If only … ?', 'What if … ?' – how often have we heard or asked these questions?

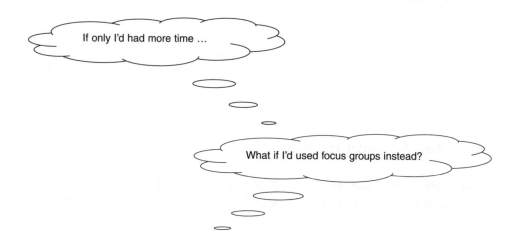

Everything has its limitations – our motivation, our focus, our interest. Whether we're in top form or struggling, these things are within our control and can be influenced to change our dissertation experience. The limitations of our study, however, are normally conditions beyond our control and so are harder to influence – for example, the data-collection period, its time constraints and its influence on the response rate.

Can you clearly and confidently answer the 'if only' or 'what if' questions? No? Then forget them; they can't change your study's findings. Simply ask yourself – what are my study's limitations? Have they any hidden benefits I could use as recommendations for consideration in future studies? Yes? Then clearly note and report.

Troubleshooting

Don't you ever wish that you knew all the challenges you'd face before starting out? Wouldn't that have made life easier? Maybe so, but really, what would you have learned about the research process? How would you improve or help others improve in future studies? So look back to feed forward.

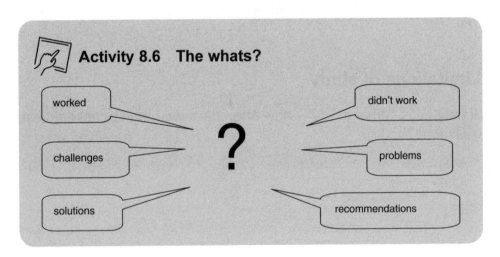

Activity 8.6   The whats?

worked
didn't work
challenges
problems
solutions
recommendations

Your dissertation toolkit

Your final year dissertation is your life's work at university, and so requires a toolkit that supports your learning style, your thinking style and your interest throughout this long process. If you don't use it then it can't help!

The visual learner's dissertation toolkit

Seeing how things fit together and develop in a big project can help motivate you and keep you focused. Chart your progress and make sense of it all by dipping into this toolkit.

- Bubbl.us
- Coloured stickers
- Dabbleboard
- Dissertation Diamond
- Exploratree
- Inspiration

- Little Book of Procrastination
- Mind Genius
- MyWebspiration
- Progress chart
- ritePen

- Sample dissertation layout – Appendix 6 on Companion Website
- Smartsheet
- Specialist software – design, film, photography, graphics
- Sticky text highlighter strips
- Storyboarding

The auditory learner's dissertation toolkit

Need to keep focused and on track when feeling the pressure? Need to hear you're on the right track and doing OK? Feel easy-to-use procedures help chart your progress? Then make good use of the practical support in your auditory toolkit.

- Background, relaxation music
- Brief journal,
- ClaroIdeas
- ClaroRead
- Coloured stickers
- Digital recorder
- Inspiration

- MyStudyBar
- Peer support
- Progress diary
- Proofreader
- Read & Write
- Sample dissertation layout – Appendix 6 on Companion Website

- Study skills tutor
- Supervisor
- Timetable
- Traffic Light System
- Turnitin
- Wall planner
- Zotero

The tactile learner's dissertation toolkit

Whether your honours project is practical or theoretical, the supports in this toolkit are useful. Work out what suits and supports your learning style so you remain motivated, focused and interested from start to finish.

- Activity book
- Arts and crafts toolbox with magnets
- Background, relaxation music
- Cardboard
- iMindMap Mobile Pro

- Journal – reflective, brief
- Mindfulness exercises
- Practical tools – design, film, photography
- Sample dissertation layout – Appendix 6 on Companion Website

- SPSS
- Stress ball
- Stress management
- Wobble board
- Worry stone

Lightning ideas

- Look at the bigger picture and see the small parts that make this up
- Tackle the small parts in small manageable chunks
- Set realistic deadlines for completing the small parts
- Prioritise and organise each part, and create your routine

- Write today's task
- Understand the task and what you need to do
- Score off deadlines task by task and check your progress
- Reward yourself, once you complete a task

- Create your data collection timelines and stick to them
- Allocate sufficient time for data analysis
- Establish a contingency plan

- Learn to say 'no' so you can tackle your task without any distractions
- Take regular breaks to relax, unwind, eat and drink
- Be confident about what you've done by writing something about your achievement each day
- Change your thinking pattern to change your progress

- Access the resources and support you need, and use them
- When you think of something, do it; don't just think about it
- Be persistent in your efforts
- Adhere to regulations – ethics, confidentiality, copyright, referencing

Hypothesise, analyse, conceptualise new knowledge

Please go to the Companion Website for this book www.sagepub.co.uk/gribben to access downloadable resources, all the activities featured here and a podcast for this chapter.

9 Referencing

This chapter looks at the art of referencing your work. It explains plagiarism and how to avoid this by following the MRTR four-step process: Managing, Recording, Thinking, Referencing.

Plagiarism – what is it exactly?	Referencing your assignments

Your referencing toolkit	Lightning ideas

Referencing – it's that thing we dread the most about our assignments. We can't really see the point of it, and, oh, trying to master the art of it gets on our nerves. It annoys even the best of us. Double-checking sources we've used is so time-consuming and if we miss out one small comma, well, we lose marks. Even worse – forget to mention an author in our assignment even though they're listed at the end, and we're penalised, even accused of plagiarism. How fair is that? All we hear is:

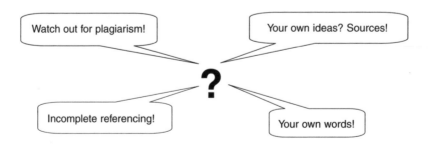

It might be their idea but it's also my idea! How can that be stealing? What's the point of it all really? The point is that if you want to quote someone or cite something, published or unpublished information, then you need to accurately acknowledge it. It's as simple as that. Otherwise, you're dabbling in plagiarism – sometimes seen as plain old stealing.

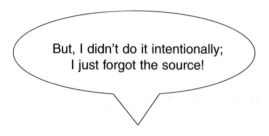

But, I didn't do it intentionally; I just forgot the source!

Maybe not, maybe so – but learn the art of referencing and you avoid the 'crime' of plagiarism, and, well, the heavy penalties that go with it.

Plagiarism – what is it exactly?

Stealing, simply forgetting to cite the source, plagiarism – call it what you like – you can't just write something that somebody else has said and not mention it's theirs. Would you like someone to take your idea and pass it off as their own just to make an assignment look good? To make them look clever? Most likely not! So search, source, read,

Table 9.1 MRTR

Managing:

- organise what and where you search
- oversee what you source
- plan the time you need for reading, thinking things over, and writing up

Thinking:

- think things through
- critically analyse what you've read to see where it fits with your own thinking and your discussion

Recording:

- list the information you want to use
- accurately note sources as you go along
- make oral summaries using a recording device

Referencing:

- reference sources accurately down to the final full stop
- check in-text citations, quotations, bibliography and all other referencing levels

note, think and then write in your own words. Most of all, make sure the quotation or citation is accurate, right down to the last comma and full stop.

Avoiding plagiarism is easy; simply follow the four-step process: Managing, Recording, Thinking, Referencing.

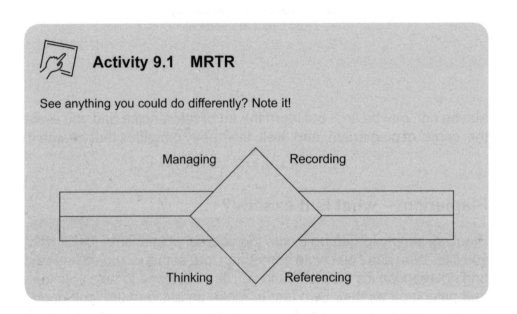

 Activity 9.1   MRTR

See anything you could do differently? Note it!

Managing   Recording

Thinking   Referencing

Activity 9.2   The 'W' questions

Use a fresh W.Cube-It (Chapter 1) for each of the following: Abbreviations; Appendices; Bibliography; Citations; Contents; Footnotes; Glossary; Indices; References.

Write the reference name, e.g. abbreviations, in the centre, and your answers to the questions below in each 'W' section:

- What's in it?
- When would you use it?
- Where do you find it?
- What's the formatting style?

Referencing your assignments

We've all come to know that the basic structure of a written assignment is traditionally: introduction, main body of discussion and conclusion. As a new student, it's enough trying to get to grips with academic writing that anything else seems too difficult. Well, referencing, acknowledging, citing – again, call it what you like – it's part of the entire package of your assignment and is something that can gain or lose you marks. So take time at the start of your studies to practise the system. Make things easier on yourself by learning it in two stages:

In-text citations

For example:

The demands of the science laboratory on the student with dyslexia are addressed by Pavey, Meehan and Waugh (2010) in their work on dyslexia-friendly post-compulsory education institutions.

Reference lists

For example:

Bird, R. (2009) *Overcoming Difficulties with Number.* London: Sage Publications.

Gathercole, S.E. and Alloway, T.P. (2008) *Working Memory and Learning.* London: Sage Publications.

McNeil, F. (2008) *Learning with the Brain in Mind.* London: Sage Publications.

Find memorising all the details difficult? Don't worry – simply check your referencing system when working on your assignments. Even the most experienced writers need to do this; it's not so unusual.

Referencing is about more than your bibliography list or what you've talked about in your assignment. It's really any added information that tells us more, that helps us to understand your discussion better, or even sparks the reader's self-interest to learn more. It's the what's in it, what's where, what more have they got to say and what does this strange language mean in your assignment:

Table 9.2   Referencing levels

Level	Detail
1 What's in it?	citations
	references
	bibliography
2 What's where?	contents
	index
3 What more have they got to say?	footnotes
	appendices
4 What does this strange language mean?	glossary
	abbreviations

Level 1: Citations, references and bibliography

Your reference list has a two-four-two (2–4–2) dimension.

It appears in two places in your assignment:

1 At relevant places within the main body of your discussion (citation)
2 At the end of your assignment (references or bibliography)

It does four things:

1 It acknowledges the sources of literature you've consulted.
2 It illustrates the extent of your reading.
3 It provides an overview of the range of literature you've consulted.
4 It lets the reader identify, locate and verify sources referred to in your discussion quickly and easily.

It consists of two types of literature sources:

1 Primary source, where you make direct reference to the work of the original author.
2 Secondary source, where you make reference to what another author says about the work of the original author.

Wondering what the difference is between citation, references and bibliography, or when to use a primary or secondary source? Not quite sure how to use these correctly in your discussion?

A citation is any source of information you refer to directly in your main discussion. This can include anything from a book or article to a film or personal correspondence in an unpublished email. In many ways, your assignment topic defines the type and range of sources you use. Using someone else's ideas or views to support your own shows you've read and considered different theories, concepts or teachings. If you summarise, paraphrase or simply refer to it in your discussion then add the author's name and date of publication in brackets. If quoting or copying directly then be sure to add the page number also.

> 'Your role is to draw your reader's attention to aspects you wish to highlight' (Sambell, Gibson and Miller, 2010, p. 100).

Your reference list is all the material you've paraphrased, summarised, quoted or directly copied in your discussion. It appears at the end of your assignment, in alphabetical order according to the author's surname. So if you cite it, acknowledge it here!

A bibliography lists all the material you've consulted to acquire background knowledge for your assignment topic, and information you've directly cited or quoted.

Don't want to lose any more valuable marks? Then check the required referencing with your tutor and follow this from the outset; different courses (and professional bodies) require different referencing styles, and not all styles separate reference and bibliography lists. Remember, you don't want to waste time and energy running around libraries to double-check references you've only half recorded or forgotten to record accurately.

Primary or secondary: when and what?

Always try to use the primary source of evidence in your assignment; that's always more impressive. Struggling to find it? Then widen your search – library, tutor, peers, internet. If the primary source is out of print or difficult to get hold of, use the secondary source, but don't forget to accurately acknowledge and reference it.

Primary:

Field (2009) provides a comprehensive and detailed overview of the world of SPSS, making it accessible and achievable even to those who fear statistics.

Secondary:

Fowler (2000, cited in Morgan and Klein, 2000, p. 204) explains why dyslexic students experience success in creative subjects such as graphic design and multi-media.

Check Harvard referencing for fuller consultation.

Books

When referencing one, two or three authors, list all names, separating by commas and the word 'and' or the symbol '&'. Be consistent: don't switch from word to ampersand symbol in the same assignment. Although there are variations in how you present the book title, italics are most commonly used. However, always check with your tutor which style they would prefer you to use, and be consistent!

One author

Ridley, D. (2008) *The Literature Review: A Step-by-Step Guide for Students*. London: Sage Publications.

Three authors

Judge, B., Jones, P., and McCreery, E. (2009) *Critical Thinking Skills for Education Students*. Exeter: Learning Matters.

Four or more authors

Use the surname of the first author only followed by 'et al.' or 'and others'.

Menter, I. et al. (2010) *A Guide to Practitioner Research in Education*. London: Sage Publications.

Journal articles

Vlachopoulos, P. and Cowan, J. (2010) Choices of approaches in e-moderation: conclusions from a grounded theory study. *Active Learning in Higher Education*, 11 (3), pp. 1–13.

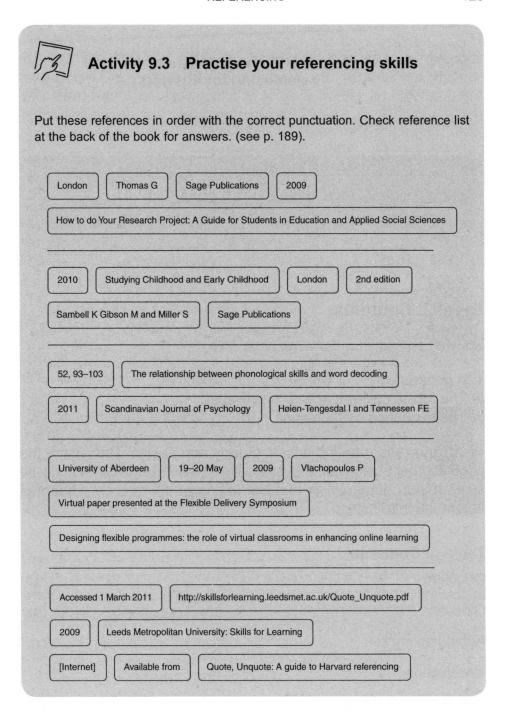

Activity 9.3   Practise your referencing skills

Put these references in order with the correct punctuation. Check reference list at the back of the book for answers. (see p. 189).

| London | Thomas G | Sage Publications | 2009 |

How to do Your Research Project: A Guide for Students in Education and Applied Social Sciences

| 2010 | Studying Childhood and Early Childhood | London | 2nd edition |

Sambell K Gibson M and Miller S   Sage Publications

| 52, 93–103 | The relationship between phonological skills and word decoding |

| 2011 | Scandinavian Journal of Psychology | Høien-Tengesdal I and Tønnessen FE |

| University of Aberdeen | 19–20 May | 2009 | Vlachopoulos P |

Virtual paper presented at the Flexible Delivery Symposium

Designing flexible programmes: the role of virtual classrooms in enhancing online learning

| Accessed 1 March 2011 | http://skillsforlearning.leedsmet.ac.uk/Quote_Unquote.pdf |

| 2009 | Leeds Metropolitan University: Skills for Learning |

| [Internet] | Available from | Quote, Unquote: A guide to Harvard referencing |

Articles from the internet

Leeds Metropolitan University: Skills for Learning (2009) Quote, Unquote: A guide to Harvard referencing [Internet]. Leeds: Leeds Metropolitan University. Available from: http://skillsforlearning.leedsmet. ac.uk/Quote_Unquote.pdf [Accessed 1 March 2011].

Activity 9.4   In-text citations (check Harvard referencing for answers)

Now practise citing these references in your assignment discussion:

1 _____

2 _____

3 _____

4 _____

5 _____

Level 2: Contents

So what should your contents page give us?

1 A general sense of what's in your assignment.
2 The topics covered in your discussion.
3 The sequence of your work.

Want your reader to find a topic quickly and easily? Then place the page number beside the relevant topic in your Table of Contents. Use small roman numerals to number pages of information presented before the introduction.

Table of Contents

Contents   i

Glossary   iii

Abbreviations list   iv

Introduction   1

Definition of dyslexia   2

Diagnosing dyslexia in adults   5

Who can diagnose?   6

Index

Want to find a particular subject quickly in a book? Then the index will give you that. It's an alphabetical list of subjects and names with their respective page numbers, found at the end of books.

Level 3: Footnotes and appendices

Footnotes

Footnotes are additional points of reference. They comment on information contained in your assignment or cite a reference related to a special part of the text; they're identified by the footnote number beside the relevant text. Footnotes tend to appear at the bottom of the page and are used in specific subjects but not in others. As Harvard referencing doesn't use footnotes, check your tutor's preferred style.

Appendices

We always want to say something more, give more information to support our views or facts, even squeeze more information into our assignment to make it look good and make us look clever. The appendices let you do that. Need to present relevant, supplementary information in a table, graph, chart, design or graphical image, but feel it's too large to include in your main discussion? Then present it as an appendix. If in doubt, check with your tutor – is your additional information included or appended? Either way, clearly label and accurately reference it.

Table 9.3   Appendices

How do I list my appendices?	alphabetically (Appendix A) or numerically (Appendix 1) – don't switch from letters to numbers in the same assignment
Where do I put them?	in two places really: • in your contents page • after your conclusion and before your reference list at the end of your assignment
Appendix or appendices – which is which?	• one appendix • two or more appendices – lists each appendix separately

Level 4: Glossary and abbreviations

Glossary: what, where, when, how

As a new student, your assignments won't include a glossary. In fact, you might never need to include a glossary in any of your course work but in case you do, you need to know what it is, and where, when and how to present it. So although your tutor discusses your research topic with you or sets the assignment and, therefore, has specialist knowledge, it's good practice to take the view that anyone reading your assignment needs to understand it without any real difficulty. So explain the strange language you use!

| What | it's a list of technical terminology in a specialised field of knowledge

---

| When | in assignments using specialist terminology: honours projects, dissertations, theses

---

| Where | it precedes your introduction but is occasionally presented at the end

---

| How | it's in alphabetical order and often in abbreviated format

---

Glossary example:

Copying – transferring information directly from one work to another

Paraphrasing – rewriting something in different words to convey the same meaning

Quoting – repeating or copying word for word what someone has said or written

Summarising – briefly outlining the main points of something

Abbreviations

Day in and day out we all read, write or use abbreviations; we're used to them, we even like them. In fact, the modern world of texting is creating abbreviations of abbreviations, producing a language of its own. Using text language in academic assignments, however, definitely isn't allowed – unless your discussion or project focuses specifically on this. Using abbreviations in some assignments dealing with specialist areas or for professional bodies, however, may be acceptable; in others though, they'd be completely misplaced. So, wondering whether you should include abbreviations in your assignment? Don't risk losing valuable marks; check what's acceptable with your tutor.

What's in an abbreviation?

1 Shortened form of a word or phrase
   a. Dr = Doctor
   b. e.g. = for example

2 Acronyms: words made from the first letters of other words
   a. SARS = Severe Acute Respiratory Syndrome
   b. NATO = North Atlantic Treaty Organisation

3 Initialisms: verbalised by letter only
   a. DVD = Digital Versatile Disc
   b. FBI = Federal Bureau of Investigation

Your referencing toolkit

The referencing toolkit should help you make sense of acknowledging other people's work in your academic assignments, so that your assignments make sense to other people.

The visual learner's referencing toolkit

Can't seem to get to grips with referencing? Then think of your learning style and shape up the referencing process. Break it down and give each part of the reference a visual shape. Picture it, think it, learn it!

• ClaroIdeas	• Mind Manager	• Shaped Post-Its
• Highlighters	• Mindview	• Sticky text highlighter strips
• Mapping Man	• Note Nuggets	• W.Cube-It

The auditory learner's referencing toolkit

Struggling to remember the steps involved in the referencing system? Why not break it down, record it and listen back with the tools in this toolkit. Hearing the process might make it stick!

• Books.google	• iPhone	• Study Buddy
• Digital recorder	• Mindmeister	• Study skills tutor
• Dragon Dictation App.	• Personal tutor	• Study Buddies bookmarks
• Endnote	• Quote, Unquote pdf	• Turnitin
• Google Scholar	• Smartphone	

The tactile learner's referencing toolkit

It's true, there are so many steps involved in referencing that the only way you feel it will sink in is by doing some practical exercises. So why not give shape and motion to your references with this toolkit.

• Academic poster	• Blackboard	• Mouse mats
• Android	• Endnote	• Referencing exercises
• Arts and crafts toolbox	• Evernote	• Walking mats
• Background, relaxation music	• Magnets	• Zotero

 Lightning ideas

- Check the referencing style used in your institution
- Refer to this when you're citing or referencing your work
- Be consistent in the system you use in the same assignment

- Use the heading 'references' or 'bibliography'
- List alphabetically according to the author's surname
- If an author isn't listed, place in alphabetical order according to the title of the work or document

---

- Keep a list of your references at the back of your assignment folder
- Record your references in a manual index card system or spreadsheet
- Avoid plagiarism – avoid cutting and pasting
- Use Turnitin

- Create a set of mind map posters listing key referencing rules, e.g. underline, bold, italics, in text-citations
- Create a visual image of your referencing system using mouse mats, walking mats or magnets
- Use the YOP code or develop your own colour-code system
- Practise referencing exercises

Write it then cite it

Please go to the Companion Website for this book www.sagepub.co.uk/gribben to access downloadable resources, all the activities featured here and a podcast for this chapter.

10 Exams

This chapter looks at exams: how to deal with things before your exams and on the exam day. It helps you organise your revision, giving you techniques for dealing with different exams. It looks at exam stress and how to switch off after your exams.

Dealing with things before your exam	Tips for revision
Dealing with things on the day of your exam	Switching off after your exam
Your exam toolkit	Lightning ideas

Exams are probably every student's biggest nightmare. It's our time to shine and show what we know but somehow exams scare us, we don't like them, they cause us major stress, but still we need to do them – and we know that. So how do we deal with the dreaded exam? Two things really – appropriate support and effective revision. Organise and prioritise things before your exam and you'll manage a successful exam process on the day.

Dealing with things before your exams

Getting support

Exams don't just happen. There's a lot of preparation from you and from others behind the scenes. It's not simply a matter of writing on your university application form that you need extra time or a PC in exams and expecting it will be in place. You need to take responsibility – talk to your Student Adviser, work out the support that suits your learning style and personality, and get any information you need to make sure everything works for you on the day. Once you do that and your support is formally recorded, the behind-the-scenes processes should run smoothly – that's their responsibility.

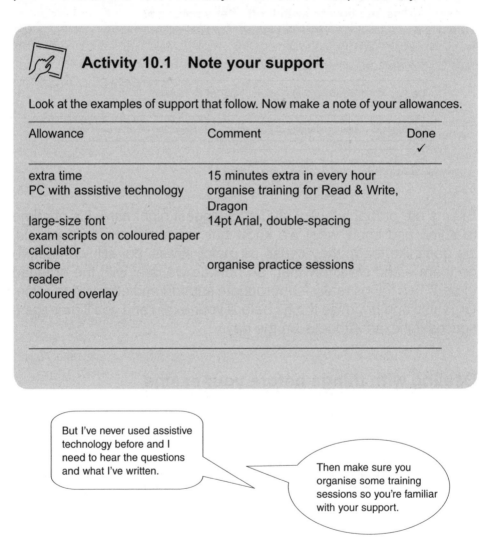

Activity 10.1   Note your support

Look at the examples of support that follow. Now make a note of your allowances.

Allowance	Comment	Done ✓
extra time	15 minutes extra in every hour	
PC with assistive technology	organise training for Read & Write, Dragon	
large-size font	14pt Arial, double-spacing	
exam scripts on coloured paper		
calculator		
scribe	organise practice sessions	
reader		
coloured overlay		

But I've never used assistive technology before and I need to hear the questions and what I've written.

Then make sure you organise some training sessions so you're familiar with your support.

If you don't follow the process, even on the day, you could end up in the main exam hall without the support you need. If you get the support but don't arrange training, then all your early preparation and hard work will have seemed like a waste of time. So be wise – don't compromise your support or your success.

Feeling anxious or stressed

Anxiety or stress is part of our DNA as a student. We carry it around in our big worry bag, but do we really need it? Well, yes and no really:

- Yes – sometimes it gives us a kick-start to get moving with our revision.
- No – at other times we foolishly let it take over and that's what we don't need when trying to revise for exams.

So know what triggers your anxiety or stress and how you cope.

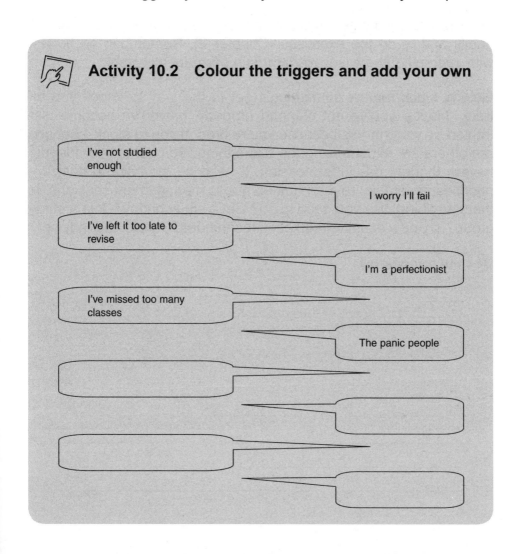

Activity 10.2   Colour the triggers and add your own

I've not studied enough

I worry I'll fail

I've left it too late to revise

I'm a perfectionist

I've missed too many classes

The panic people

Look at the jagged space between the speech bubbles. Can you see the stress line? How does it make you feel? That you'll succeed or fail? So what needs to change? Have you thought about stress management sessions, revision workshops – anything else?

Putting things off or getting stuck

Ever find you plan well, are full of good intentions but something else just seems to get in the way? Find you keep putting off getting started? Feel you start revising, get distracted, feel stuck and don't quite know how to get back on track? We've all been there at some point; we know how it feels, but stop! Stop making excuses or looking for reasons to convince yourself that everything's all right.

Putting off starting your revision or getting stuck after you've started are two different things. Putting it off? Then revisit your procrastination habits and re-do the exercises (Chapter 2). Remember, be honest with yourself. Otherwise, you'll remain permanently stuck!

Getting stuck means something's got in the way to knock you off track. Maybe you've not planned properly, or you've become distracted by your nerves because you're tired. If you're stuck, chances are others are experiencing the same thing. So chat to your friends; have a thought de-clutter session. If need be, go back to basics – priorities, timetable, revision folder, stress management sessions. Is there anything else you need to do? Get a study buddy? Join a study group? Try new exam or relaxation techniques? Talk to your adviser?

De-clutter storyboard

Avoid putting off or getting stuck by being realistic about what's achievable in any given day. Don't overload yourself and don't over-think; stick to your original plan and make good use of the support you need.

Knowing about your actual exam

Different types of exams require different things; some shorter answers, others longer. How often do we carry on studying, not checking exactly what type of exam we'll have to take, and then stress when the unexpected happens? So knowing your exam structure early on should help you to organise and structure your revision. It's key to your success.

Remember all the practical things – when and where are your exams? How long are they? How long will it take you to get to your exam location? When will you get your results?

Tips on revision

Essay-type exams

Traditionally, we expect to answer essay-type questions in our exams. Nowadays, however, there's more option and variety in assessment methods. Sometimes we get to choose how we'd like to be assessed; something that suits our learning style. Nevertheless, essay-type exams will probably always be part and parcel of our assessment process.

Writing an essay in an exam is slightly different from what's expected in a continuous assessment assignment. For a start, an exam essay is much shorter and less detailed. So you're not expected to list references at the end, include accurate citations in your discussion or even footnotes. Remember that writing under timed conditions is different. So, use past papers to practise and manage your time.

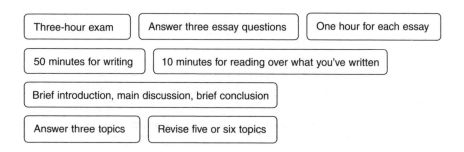

Three-hour exam   Answer three essay questions   One hour for each essay

50 minutes for writing   10 minutes for reading over what you've written

Brief introduction, main discussion, brief conclusion

Answer three topics   Revise five or six topics

Don't make the mistake of learning an essay off by heart with the hope of writing it in your exam, or revising three topics only. If the topics you've studied don't come up then you've wasted your time and this may trigger exam panic. What you need to trigger is information recall, so highlight key points when practising essay writing and work on your academic language style; don't use chatty language (Chapter 7).

Multiple-choice exams

Multiple-choice exams – we either love them or we hate them. So many answers, too many choices; what do we do? If your course deals with lots of factual information then you'll surely come across multiple-choice exams. So learn the method, learn your subject and you'll know how to tackle them. You may even surprise yourself by actually liking them!

The method

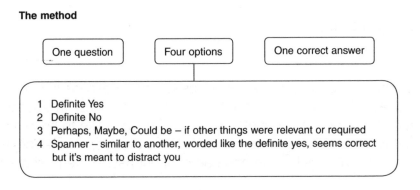

By adding the Spanner, your tutor isn't trying to catch you out; it's all about your knowledge and your decision-making abilities. So trust the method and your own instinct when unpacking the answer.

The 5-Step answer finder

Read the question, cover up the answers and try to recall the answer in your head

Then read all the answers

Rule in, rule out – look at answers one by one and get rid of the Definite No

Look for the opposites and rule out the Perhaps, if only other things were relevant

Work out why the Spanner is exactly that, and rule it out

So you have your answer. If you're still unsure, trust your instinct and guess the answer. Who knows, you could be correct and gain a valuable mark!

 Activity 10.3   Symbol association

Use symbols that mean something to you to help work out the answer

Definite Yes	
Definite No	
Perhaps; Maybe; Could be	
Spanner	

Revise with a friend and test your knowledge:

- practise the ruling in and ruling out method using past papers
- devise a ruling in and ruling out method that works for you
- write your own multiple-choice papers.

While you can control your timing in hard-copy paper multiple-choice exams, online exams can be different. What you need to know:

- How long is the exam and how many questions does it contain?
- Can you go back and change an answer at any time?
- Do you need to save each answer as you go along?
- Can you partially complete the exam and return to it later?
- Can you print out the exam paper, work out your answers and then answer online?
- Can you answer the easy questions first?

During the exam, avoid disturbances:

- Tell your family it's exam time.
- Make a 'do not disturb' notice.
- Switch off your mobile, social networking site or electronic games.

Short-answer exams

If you're studying on a practitioner-based course, you'll often come across short-answer exams: concise questions that require concise and, quite often, factual answers. Want to know how long your answer should be? Then use the marks allocated to the question as a guide for the number of points you need to give.

Example:

Name the two types of communication

2 marks

This question is looking for two points to describe communication, so don't launch into writing several paragraphs or produce a half-page answer.

Revise with a friend and test your knowledge:

- Practise a selection of short-answer questions from past papers.
- Use your lecture notes to prepare your own short-answer questions.

Practical exams

Some subjects such as Nursing and Music have practical exams. Don't ignore the fact that you also need to revise for these. Practice makes perfect and builds confidence. It improves your practitioner abilities and sets you up for a good pass mark, so allocate time to prepare. Work with a friend, make notes, map the steps, check your timing and your sequencing, and give feedback. If you're unsure and struggling with any part of the practical tasks, ask your tutor for advice and clarification.

Practical points to remember:

1 Know that instructions are generally provided.
2 Follow each instruction in the correct order.
3 Don't rush the process.

Where to start – organise to revise

With revision time on the horizon, organising your days and weeks should give you the balance needed to confidently revise.

Activity 10.4   Your bigger picture

What's in yours? Note down the items and the time needed for each.

What makes up your student day?	What are your family commitments?
What are your work commitments?	What exams do you need to revise?

Now step back, look at the bigger picture and your new revision commitments. Feel you need to amend the amount of time spent on these? Why not start with your current timetable – what stays and what goes leading up to the exams? Build in some 'me' time so you strike a balance between work and relaxation. Take a day off to relax your mind and body; re-energise yourself and your revision with new commitment, focus and concentration.

Activity 10.5   Revision hours

You know your timetable, you know the priorities, and you know when and where you study best. Now identify when you'll revise; place your schedule on your study notice board, in your phone reminder or in your study folder.

Day of the week	a.m.	p.m.
Sunday		
Monday		
Tuesday		
Wednesday		
Thursday		
Friday		
Saturday		

Now let's sort out your revision folder. Let's face it – you don't really want to carry around four or five different folders just to revise. One's enough, with subject dividers to separate your topics. So what do you need?

Table 10.1   Your revision notes

lecture notes	essays
tutorial notes	handouts
seminar notes	past papers
personal reading notes	reading list
study group notes	discussion board notes
study buddy notes	reflective journal notes
logbook notes	storyboards

Now you're not going to carry around all of this either. Make your folder lighter and your revision smoother by following weeks 1–6 in the build-up-countdown table.

Building up and counting down

Effective revision is all about planning, timing and using revision techniques that suit your learning style. So build up your subject knowledge to count down effectively to exams. Don't make yourself restless and insecure by continuously looking for new material. Be confident that you've more than enough to pass your exams!

Table 10.2   Revision countdown

Weeks 1–6	• make notes from old notes, linear notes, lists, sections, sub-sections, bullet points, mnemonics, copy formulae, facts and figures
	• use colour, symbols, patterns, shapes, graphical images
	• gather new information
Weeks 6–7	• arrange a study group, study buddy, discussion board
	• start revision
	• create mind maps, Mapping Man, storyboards
Weeks 8–10	• practise past papers
	• write summaries, tables, charts
Weeks 11–13	• use flashcards
	• listen to recorded notes
Weeks 14–15	• exams start
	• eat, sleep and relax well

Copying

Create new notes from old ones; copy information, highlight, colour, add symbol association, chunk information.

Using a digital recorder

Listening helps make information recall easier:

- record your notes
- listen while reading your notes
- listen to your notes before going to sleep.

Index cards

Revise anytime, anywhere with easy-to-use portable index cards:

- write the key points on one side of the card
- write a brief explanation or summary on the other side.

Mind mapping

Use the Mapping Man, W. Cube-It (Chapter 1) or create your own poster-size mind map to jot down key information:

- use different colours for different subjects
- write down key points and develop these
- write down a summary of the topic at the bottom of your mind map.

Mnemonics

You either love them or you hate them but they're particularly useful if you need to learn specialist terminology. Take the first letter of each key point to make your mnemonic word or phrase – for example PIE = part of the inner ear. Why not create your own mnemonic storyboard dictionary?

Shape association

Shape up your ideas, shape up your revision and shape up your visual recall in exams! Adapt the shaping up your ideas system in Chapter 7's 'dealing with writer's block' to suit your revision learning style.

Post-revision – pre-exam

Revision over? Don't relax just yet! There's some final preparation to do; things you need to check before your exam day to make sure everything runs smoothly. Not quite sure how you get your allowances on the day of the exam? Then check it out with your exam office or with Student Services well in advance.

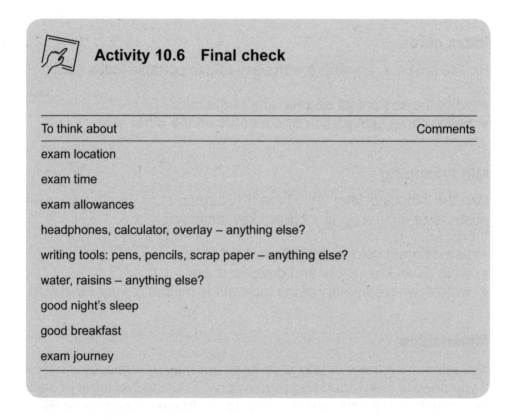

Activity 10.6   Final check

To think about	Comments
exam location	
exam time	
exam allowances	
headphones, calculator, overlay – anything else?	
writing tools: pens, pencils, scrap paper – anything else?	
water, raisins – anything else?	
good night's sleep	
good breakfast	
exam journey	

There's nothing worse than finding you've run out of ink, forgotten your pencil sharpener or getting extremely thirsty during your exam. Remember, you need to take more than a sharp mind into the exam room. So remember the tools you'll need as well as a good night's sleep.

Dealing with things on the day of your exam

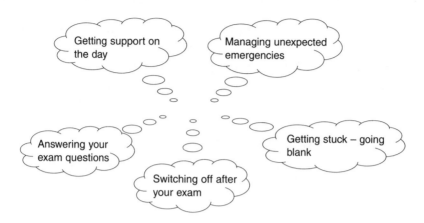

Getting support on the day

Managing unexpected emergencies

Answering your exam questions

Switching off after your exam

Getting stuck – going blank

Getting support on the day

Arranging support is important but making sure you get what you need on the day, you'll agree, is equally important. Make sure you know exactly how to get your exam support on the day. Otherwise, you'll end up in the same exam hall as everyone else and the distractions there could be a sure recipe for disaster! So on the day, double-check:

- your allowances are in place and everything functions
- you're in the correct exam room
- you've got all the working tools you need and they function.

Place what you need on the desk in front of you. Don't distract others or yourself by fumbling around in your bag for something you've forgotten. Switch off your mobile!

Managing unexpected emergencies

We're more than just a student; we're married, have children or are part of a wider family. Things happen to them, to us and most often when we least expect them. We can't legislate for unexpected emergencies but knowing how to deal with them should make things easier and less stressful. So make sure you understand the mitigation process at your university; check out the details on your student website and inform your tutor or adviser as soon as your emergency happens.

If your mitigation is a little more complex and you need some extra time to complete your studies, this can be arranged. Needing extra time because of an emergency isn't so unusual. It's better to have this than put unnecessary pressure on yourself and potentially fail.

Of course, then there are the other emergencies where you're late for the exam because you've overslept, missed a bus, run out of petrol, been caught in traffic, forgotten your matriculation card or pencil case. So make sure you know who to call if anything like that happens. If you turn up late, don't rush in noisily and disturb others; be quiet and discreet.

Answering your exam questions

Make good use of your extra time. Don't rush into completing your exam paper without:

- checking you've got the correct exam paper
- completing your personal details
- reading the general exam instructions carefully
- checking and highlighting the number of exam questions you must answer
- reading the entire exam paper
- selecting and highlighting the questions you want to answer
- highlighting the key asking words – making sure you understand the question
- feeling confident about your choice
- jotting down and drawing a line under your initial ideas at the top of your answer booklet page
- timing each answer
- feeling relaxed before writing.

Remember, you can answer the questions in any order you want. It's always best and easiest, though, if you start with the one you've studied best, feel most confident about and enjoy.

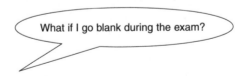

What if I go blank during the exam?

Getting stuck – going blank

Whatever you do, don't panic! That will only make matters worse. If you're struggling with the first question, simply:

- leave that question
- do your relaxation techniques

- move on to the next question
- jot down ideas to help jog your memory
- return to the first question later.

Don't worry if you're unable to return to the question – the examiner will see from your notes what you intended to answer.

Switching off after your exam

We're all guilty of it and yet still we do it; why, oh, why do we torture ourselves by talking about the exam just as soon as we've left the exam room? We huddle around like a closed meeting telling each other the questions we answered, how hard or easy we found them, what we'd wished we'd answered instead, whether we feel we've done well or not, whether we ran out of time, and, oh, the panic that sets in if we think we've messed up. How horrible we feel, if we think someone's got it right and we've got it wrong. We don't do ourselves any favours, do we?

So, exam over, let's put it behind you. It's over; you can't do anything to change your response or the mark you're given, so close the exam door and move on. Remember, you prepared well, you did your best, and while talking about it can be helpful in some ways for some of you, perhaps confirming your responses and so boosting your confidence, that's not always the case. Don't set yourself on the worry path; it's not worth it. Keep your energy to prepare for your next exam. Make a habit of finding a way to switch off, re-charge your batteries and re-focus.

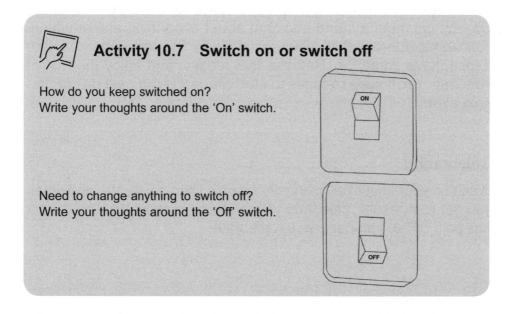

Activity 10.7   Switch on or switch off

How do you keep switched on?
Write your thoughts around the 'On' switch.

ON

Need to change anything to switch off?
Write your thoughts around the 'Off' switch.

OFF

Re-charging and re-focusing

Found that relaxation music and techniques worked for you before the exam? Then they'll surely benefit you now. Create some thinking space so you're prepared for the next exam.

Stress-buster activities

Feel you need to unwind? Need less talk and more walk? Then release the exam tension from your mind and body by doing some physical activity: go to the gym, go for a run, power walk, swim, dance, or team up with others for some sporting activity. Work off the stress to feel mentally and physically refreshed.

Distraction activities

Want to close the exam door behind you and move on? Then do something that distracts you from turning things over in your mind and fuelling unnecessary worry. Arrange a shopping trip with a friend, visit an art gallery or museum, go to the movies or do some handicrafts. Avoid the negatives by practising some self-affirmation – think positive!

Coffee chatter

Who doesn't enjoy meeting up for a coffee and a chat? We all do! So why not meet a friend and chat about everything and anything. Talk about your holidays, your social life for the week ahead, share a joke, have some fun. Release that tension and enjoy the rest of your day. You'll soon re-focus to start preparing the next day for the next exam.

Celebrating

Was this your final ever university exam? Then celebrate, and when you get your results, celebrate your success in style! Your hard work has paid off, so you deserve to celebrate.

Your exam toolkit

We all need pointers and help when trying to revise for exams. We need to do it our way, as what works for one won't work for another. So test out the different tools in your exam toolkit. Find what works for you and enjoy your revision and your exams.

The visual learner's exam toolkit

Find it easier to recall information through pictures, images, colour? Feel the information sticks better? Then this toolkit is ideal for you.

• ClaroIdeas	• Mapping Man	• Study Buddies bookmarks
• ClaroRead	• MyStudyBar	• Thought pots
• Highlighters	• Note Nuggets	• Timetable
• Index cards	• Read & Write	• W.Cube-It
• Inspiration	• Storyboarding	• Wisemapping

The auditory learner's exam toolkit

Want to aid your information recall in exams? Then listen to your exam notes by using the tools in this toolkit.

• Audio notetaker	• Google Scholar	• Personal tutor
• Background, relaxation music	• Livescribe Echo Pen	• Read & Write
• ClaroRead	• iPhone	• Reader
• Digital recorder	• iTunesU podcasts	• Study Buddy
• Dragon Dictation App.		

The tactile learner's exam toolkit

Actively doing things when it comes to exam time helps take care of the nerves. Why not use these tools to help with revision, memory recall and exam stress.

- Blackboard
- Hypnotherapy
- Mindfulness exercises
- Moodle

- Progress chart
- Relaxation techniques
- Revision folder
- Sports

- Stress ball
- Study group
- Walking mat

🔆 Lightning ideas

- Decide when you study best
- Draw up a revision timetable and stick to it
- Revise in short spells
- Don't study for more than 45 minutes without taking a break

- Rotate the subjects you study every hour
- Keep track of your revision with pop-up reminders or timer
- Organise and use one revision folder

- Use a study buddy
- Practise with your scribe
- Do relaxation techniques
- Do some physical activities

- Switch off distractions – mobile, social networking, games
- Use text-to-speech software for revision
- Record your exam notes
- Listen to your exam notes just before you go to sleep

- Organise your exam support
- Make a note of your exam room
- Organise all you need to use on the exam day
- Plan your exam day journey

- Eat well and sleep well, particularly the night before the exam
- Don't revise into the small hours
- Don't skip breakfast on your exam day

Smart start, successful finish

 Please go to the Companion Website for this book www.sagepub.co.uk/gribben to access downloadable resources, all the activities featured here and a podcast for this chapter.

11 Oral Presentations

This chapter looks at oral presentations. Using the Presentation Pyramid, it takes you through the steps involved in good oral presentation preparation and delivery, from initial planning to the live presentation.

> Presentation Pyramid from planning to newsreel

> Difficult dealings

> Your presentations toolkit

> Lightning ideas

Individual or in groups, presentations are fast becoming part and parcel of our academic assessment processes. Whether it's giving information to support our written work or introducing a new topic, feeling confident and in command of our presentation when we go 'live' in front of our class or tutors requires preparation. How often have we heard 'it's all in the preparation' and not taken it seriously? Taking time to plan and prepare from the outset can make the difference between delivering a good or bad presentation, a pass or fail, and a confidence boost or knock! So being aware of the subtle differences between a good or bad presentation is key to your preparation process.

A good presentation should:

- be well prepared and structured so you're confident when presenting
- be given in a clear voice with regular thinking pauses
- send crisp, clear messages
- be effective, engaging and inquisitive
- anticipate the questions
- keep to the time limit and be delivered timely.

A bad presentation generally:

- contains too many slides, overloaded with too much detail
- doesn't generate many questions
- bores or switches off the audience
- is unclear and uninspiring
- runs significantly over time
- rambles on in a rushed, monotonous voice.

Also central to your preparation process is the presentation's purpose, audience, topic, type, and duration; they set its tone. Table 11.1 sets out some oral presentation examples.

Table 11.1   Presentation types

Purpose	Audience	Topic	Type	Duration (Mins)
complete learning outcome	tutor, class, internal examiner	pre-school play therapy	oral (individual, group, pairs)	20 30
defend written work	tutor, internal examiner	human rights	oral retrieval (individual)	15
complete learning outcome	tutor, class, internal examiner	business banking	oral – poster (individual, group, pairs)	15 30
support written work	tutor, class, internal examiner	sport and mental health	oral – film; storyboard (individual, group, pairs)	15 30
support written work	tutor, class, internal examiner	landscape technology	oral – photos (individual)	15
support written work	tutor, class, internal examiner	global communication	podcast, vodcast (individual)	15
complete learning outcome	tutor, class, internal examiner	the learning corner	oral – design artefact; storyboard (individual)	15

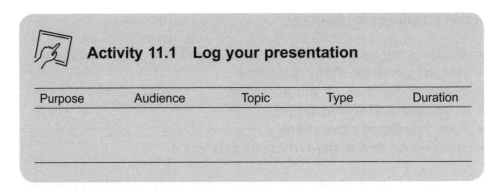

Activity 11.1   Log your presentation

Purpose	Audience	Topic	Type	Duration

Although different presentation types carry different marking criteria and weightings, and demand a different focus or approach, the preparation principles are the same. Working through the different steps in the Presentation Pyramid should help you to keep focused, organised and on track to meet expectations and achieve learning outcomes.

Presentation Pyramid from planning to newsreel

The Presentation Pyramid takes you through the different steps involved in preparing a good presentation. On your own or in a group, tailor the Pyramid to suit your needs. Work with friends who'll give moral support and reassurance about your content and approach.

Planning

Giving a good and memorable presentation is on every student's wish list. We all want our presentation to be remembered for the right reasons:

and not for the blunders or uninspiring quality:

It's all in the delivery ... if only you'd prepared better.

Good planning provides structure to what's required for delivering a good and memorable presentation, not only for the right reasons but also for a good pass mark. So, if you take time to plan and prepare well then you'll surely deliver well. You have the topic, you know your subject and you like to talk. Oh, but don't let the nerves get in the way. Even the most experienced lecturers can get nervous; we've all experienced that; it's not so unusual. Just remember, being prepared practically and emotionally means good delivery, so tackle the nerves and factor in some therapeutic support. When allocating tasks, plan, decide and work out the detail together, and play to individual strengths:

- presentation content – specific subject areas
- timetable for tasks – realistic, manageable and frequent 'touching base' deadlines
- who does what – task and subject, slide presentation order, frequent checklisting
- presentation layout – PowerPoint, mind map, poster, storyboard
- additional information – handouts, subject-related artefacts, practical activity tools
- storing the information – mind map, index files, poster, audio
- discussing the presentation – online discussion room, webcam, texting, study group, tweeting
- support – student adviser consultation, practice sessions, stress management, alternative therapy.

With the detail planned, set up your discussion board pyramids, sort the topics and create a Talking Corner for comments. Simply add information from the point of research.

Activity 11.2 Pyramid planning

Use one pyramid for each presentation task: planning, researching, evaluating, sorting, energising, noting, talking, anticipating, timing, illustrating, oral practice, newsreel

Part of the planning is to anticipate that different personalities might not work effectively as a group. Need to change groups to do so? Then change early on. You can and you must, if good presentation delivery is your focus.

Researching

At this early point, you might well say:

Researching? It's only a presentation not a dissertation!

Yes, but even presentations require some research. Remember, it's not just a matter of standing up in class and talking off the top of your head. Show your audience that your presentation is considered, balanced and well thought through. Prove you're in command of your topic; that you know what you're talking about. Let them see you can answer questions confidently and knowledgeably. With this in mind, let's research …

Why not start with your lecture, tutorial, seminar notes? Most of the information you need should be there. Check out the topic, the specific subjects related to that area and use coloured arrow Post-its as bookmarks to highlight where to find what you need. If you're dealing with a new topic then you'll need to widen your search: library, internet, audio books, e-journals, newspapers, magazines, reports. Anything else?

If someone in your group is excellent at internet searches and another isn't then it makes sense to remember the strengths and allocate to annotate effectively. This should keep the group on task and on target.

Evaluating

Researching and gathering information gives a great sense of achievement and why not? It's all there, now it's a matter of evaluating what you've gathered. Say 'yes' or 'no' to what you feel you need to use, to what's relevant. Be quick and decisive in your first evaluation; don't indulge in time wasting. You can always endorse your decision by revisiting these lists as a group. As the presentation takes some shape, new ideas crop up and decisions become clearer.

- create a Yes and No list
- record specific subjects, sources and Where to find What index cards (see Table 1.2)
- put the No list to the side but don't discard it just yet; you might use something later
- highlight the Yes information in your notes.

Sorting

Now sort the information in your What Belongs Where Pyramids of the group discussion board:

- topic then individual subjects
- subject sections and sub-sections
- subject categories and sub-categories
- graphical detail
- comments.

Sorting in this way lets you see both the bigger picture and the finer detail, and gives you an idea of how the presentation should develop and unfold. You can add and subtract, condense sections and categories, and re-think and re-shape your ideas. Considering the topic, ask yourself: What does the audience need to know? What's additional information? What's your message? Be clear about that and your start-to-finish thread – from topic to key points, to message, to discussion, to enquiring minds – will become clear.

Energising

Although you're still in the process of sorting information and putting things together, it's never too early to consider the 'going live' side of a presentation – your body language, attitude, voice, verbal language, signposting and timing. How you present yourself establishes your

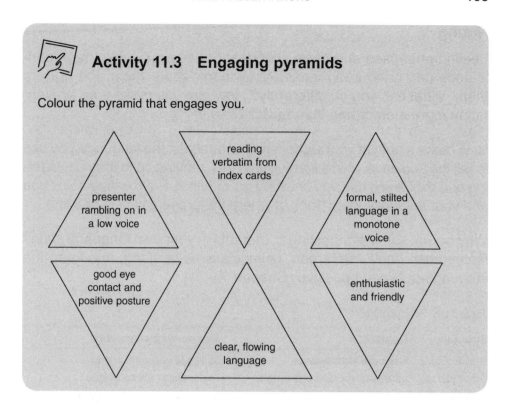

Activity 11.3   Engaging pyramids

Colour the pyramid that engages you.

- reading verbatim from index cards
- presenter rambling on in a low voice
- formal, stilted language in a monotone voice
- good eye contact and positive posture
- enthusiastic and friendly
- clear, flowing language

credibility! So ask yourself: What engages you in presentations? What holds your attention? What energises you when you're part of the audience? Or … what switches you off?

Will you switch on or switch off your audience? Remember, presentations don't need to be perfect. They can't be, if you want to come across as natural as possible. Sure, things can go wrong; the unexpected can happen, but if you energise yourself then you'll energise your audience and the memorable presentation will take over. Think positively! With your preparation on track, get your presentation skills on track by working with your:

- student adviser > alleviate your stress, build your confidence
- tutor > learn about voice control and timing
- friend > re-vitalise your body language.

Take the feedback, breathe new life into it, energise it, do something different, and put your own personal stamp on your presentation.

Noting

Feeling energised and more confident? Let's pass it on. Fresh confidence can bring fresh ideas. Note them, share them and nurture them. What can you do differently? How can you make your presentation more memorable than most? Note it!

Now make a note of your signposting comments: the language you use to tell the audience you're starting with this, moving on to that, considering and explaining this and finishing up with that. Signposting helps you and your audience keep track of where the presentation is heading.

Why not list some signposting comments in your own language style? Remember, don't use jargon, colloquialisms or slang, and keep the language active not passive (Chapter 7).

Table 11.2   Signposting

Structure	Content	Signposting comments
introduction (what you're going to talk about)	welcome the audience introduce yourself and others introduce your topic and structure say how you'll handle questions	I'd like to welcome you to ... I'm ... this is my colleague ... today, we'd like to talk about ... we'll take questions at the end ...
main (talk about it)	topics and specific subjects	first of all, let's look at ... now moving on to ... just to illustrate this point ... a good example is ... the significance here ...
conclusion (what you've said)	summing up references recommendations	just to re-cap on ... if you're interested, check out ... you might want to consider ...
discussion (chatting about it; answer now or follow up on later)	questions and answers	you raise some interesting issues here that affect ... would anyone else have anything to say about ... I'm not sure I quite grasp that, can you repeat it, please ... sorry, I don't know the answer to that right now – can I get back to you when I've checked out the details ...
sign off (your appreciation)	acknowledge and thank audience	thank you for listening ... thanks for your questions ...

Talking

While online discussion rooms allow you to touch base with your group anytime, anywhere, meeting up can generate a whole new preparation process. What you put into this session is what you'll get out of it. So, free from family or other distractions, teamwork means you can:

- collectively see a visual image of the presentation content
- hear ideas, suggestions and comments at the same time
- generate new ideas from others' ideas
- discuss points thoroughly
- reach decisions quicker
- check progress and future process
- decide on final layout
- provide moral support.

Want to get the most out of your session? Then why not make it fun by building an outsized pyramid on the table or floor. Colour it, label it, even signpost it and get a feel for its message. Alternatively, use the 3-D organiser Topicscape. This should enhance the brainstorming and decision-making. Feeling happy with your decisions? Then confidently disregard the 'No' list now.

Anticipating

Ever attended a presentation where the presenter panicked when asked an awkward question?

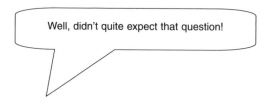

Well, didn't quite expect that question!

This isn't something you want to hear in a presentation, let alone have to say. So anticipate the questions. Draw up at least two obvious questions for each key point you make, and one not so obvious question, and prepare your answer. Why not recall some of the questions you asked throughout your preparation process. Is there anything else you'd like to know?

Anticipating the question means you'll feel in command of the message you want to get across. If you can't answer a question, whatever you do, don't bluff it; just say you'll come back to it.

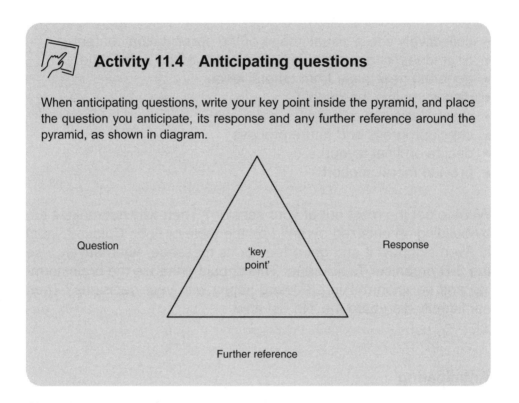

Activity 11.4   Anticipating questions

When anticipating questions, write your key point inside the pyramid, and place the question you anticipate, its response and any further reference around the pyramid, as shown in diagram.

Question

'key point'

Response

Further reference

Timing

How often have you listened to a presentation where too much time's been spent on one point and not enough on another; where everything's been so rushed that you leave the room none the wiser about the key message?

Get the timing right for tasks and you'll have pretty much worked out your pace of delivery. Knowing how long the presentation is will help you work out the content – how many slides, bullet points, illustrations, activities – and how long you should spend introducing, discussing and concluding the topic. Oh, and don't forget the question and answer session at the end. Know when to stop taking questions. If you let this drag on, the audience may just forget your impressive presentation!

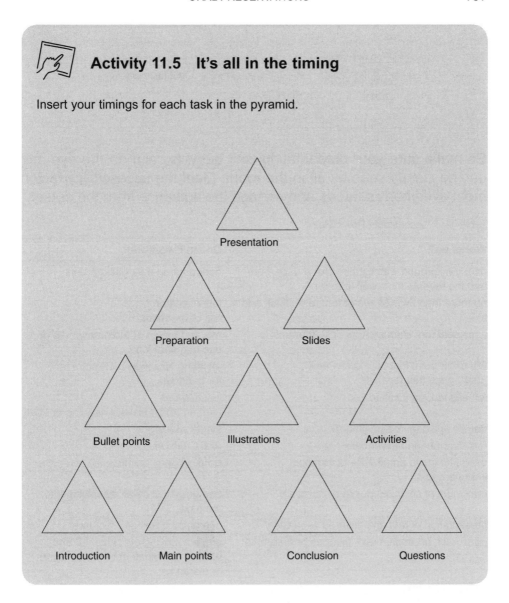

Activity 11.5 It's all in the timing

Insert your timings for each task in the pyramid.

Presentation

Preparation   Slides

Bullet points   Illustrations   Activities

Introduction   Main points   Conclusion   Questions

Illustrating

Putting the final touches to your PowerPoint presentation means you're almost 'good to go'. You've reached that point where graphics can be added to support your factual information or reinforce any points you've made. Remember, if they're not clearly detailed and relevant, they're simply a visual 'add on'. So don't include distraction that detracts from an otherwise brilliant presentation. Oh, and don't forget the accessibility factor! Think of what you often complain about. What would you do differently?

So make sure your presentation isn't busy, is calm on the eye and can be clearly seen by all in the room. Meet the accessibility factor, meet everybody's needs and engage the audience from the outset.

Table 11.3   Accessible PowerPoint

Works well	Doesn't work well
dark background with light text for a dark room and the reverse for a well-lit room	dark print on dark background
no more than two colours of font, e.g. black and blue	lots of colour red or green text
sans serif font such as Arial or Verdana	mix and match of too many fonts or use of a serif font
28- or 32-point font for PowerPoint 30-40-point font for OHP	anything less than a 12-point font for handouts
left aligned, un-justified text	justified text centred text (unless a heading or title)
double spacing (1.5 minimum)	single spacing
mix of upper and lower case	ALL CAPITALS
use of boxes to emphasise or highlight important text	**bold,** <u>underline</u>, *italics*
maximum of six bullet points or numbers	one graphical detail dissolving into the next
presentation of text and pictures separately	overlapping text and pictures
horizontal, un-angled text, pictures or diagrams	angled, moving or horizontal and vertical combination of text, pictures or diagrams
clear, visible text on diagrams, graphs or tables	overuse of animation
use of visuals instead of text where possible	floating or moving text

Remember your own accessibility. You need to be able to clearly read your prompt cards, so keep them as bare as possible.

Table 11.4   Accessible prompt cards

Do	Don't
use clear bullet points	overload text and references
give brief additional information	cram up annotations
use clear highlighting colours or symbols	use too many colours or symbols
match card numbers with PowerPoint slides	use unnumbered cards

Oral practice

Want to avoid adverse comments? Want to hear how it all sounds before going 'live'? Want to see that you can do it, despite the nerves? Then get in some oral practice: alone in front of a mirror, with your friends, family or tutor. Remove the unfamiliarity and anxiety, particularly if you're being recorded (video or audio) for external marking. Practise, so you're not thrown by:

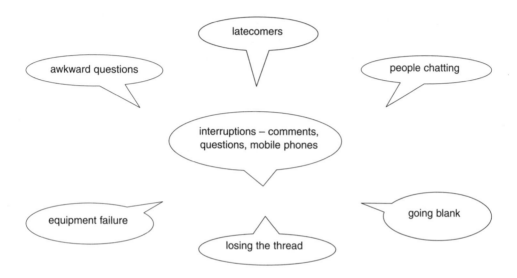

Practice gives you:

- a chance to check delivery: timing, pace, voice projection and command of information
- confirmation of structure and detail
- confidence in answering questions
- a sense of familiarity with use of technology
- a sense of moral support and re-assurance
- a feeling of being well prepared
- a sense of achievement
- self-belief
- less worry when dealing with an unfamiliar situation
- a minimisation of stress on the actual day
- a gauge of the 'temperature' of the audience and establishes rapport quickly

- positive 'live' presentation
- confidence to deal with the unexpected.

If you don't practise, you'll:

- add to your anxiety when going 'live'
- detract from your ability to deliver fluently and timely
- be disadvantaged rather than on an even footing with those who've practised
- struggle to engage the audience
- rely more on your prompt cards
- easily lose the thread of your message
- appear ill-prepared.

Newsreel

You've noted the information, nurtured the discussion, prepared the slides and handouts, and you've worked on the nerves; now it's time for the live presentation. Before going 'live', however, make sure you do a final check the day before. Is everything functional and 'good to go'?

 Activity 11.6   Final checklist

Things to organise	Done (✓)
location	
room layout	
correct equipment	
functional and familiar technology	
practical activity or demonstration items	
personal support tools: prompt cards, water, clock, handouts, artefacts	
anything else?	

OK, check done – let's roll!

1 Place your water and prompt cards within easy reach, and discreetly, so they don't distract you or your audience.
2 Stand firmly to the left or right of your PowerPoint – wherever you feel most comfortable and confident to deliver; don't stand in front of it and block the audience view.
3 Place your first slide up and signpost the presentation.
4 Scan the room, re-focus on one person who appears positive and interested and begin; look at your slide, present your first point and scan back to your audience; don't focus completely, or for long spells, on one person.
5 Remember to show you're in command of what you're talking about by keeping check of your body language, voice tone and pitch.
6 Check your timing so it doesn't seem too formal or rehearsed.
7 Refer to your PowerPoint; don't rely too much on your prompt cards.

Difficult dealings

- If the unexpected happens during the 'live' presentation, make sure you've a strategy to get you through. Ask your friends about their personal strategies, and practise.
- Losing the thread – confidently re-cap on previous bullet points and check the signposting. If you lose track completely, apologise, check the PowerPoint and discreetly refer to your prompt card notes.
- Going blank – if your presentation is interesting, your audience probably won't notice you've gone blank, so don't panic. If you're feeling stuck, however, stimulate your recall by confidently re-capping on the last bullet point, discreetly referring to your prompt card, or asking the audience if they've any questions at that point (see Chapter 2 for additional 'going blank' information).
- Difficult questions – why not return a difficult question with a question or open it up to the audience to respond? You could also

choose to answer the question or say you'll deal with it later. The decision is yours but remain confident!

- Disinterested audience – don't be put off by someone in the audience who appears unhappy. If you look interesting and smile, it just might rub off!

Your presentation toolkit

The presentation toolkit is simple and easy to use. Whether you're a novice or an old hand at oral presentations, simply combine the Presentation Pyramid with useful strategies you've learned from earlier chapters and adapt your own techniques.

The visual learner's presentation toolkit

Want to engage your visual thinking to your learning? Want to see your presentation developing and unfolding? Want to collaboratively brainstorm in real time? Then use these tools to capture your brainwaves and picture your thoughts for easy editing and sharing.

- Arrow Post-its
- Dabbleboard
- Flipchart
- Highlighters
- Mindmeister
- OHPs
- PowerPoint
- Presentation Pyramid
- Storyboarding
- Topicscape

The auditory learner's presentation toolkit

Want to share thoughts in real-time? Need to hear the good or bad in your delivery? Then dip into this toolkit. The variety of tools allows you to capture, discuss, edit and share information.

- Audacity
- Camtasia
- Digital recorder
- Index cards
- Mp3
- Notebook
- Personal tutor
- PowerPoint audio input
- Prompt cards
- Skype
- Student Adviser
- Study group
- Twitter
- Webcam

The tactile learner's presentation toolkit

Feel the preparation process evolving and taking shape by creating your own floor-size Presentation Pyramid. Using these tools can help provide some deeper thinking and learning, control your nerves and sharpen your presentation skills.

- Arts and crafts toolbox
- Background, relaxation music
- Body language workshops
- Cardboard

- Highlighters
- Hypnotherapy
- Mindfulness exercises
- Practical activity tools
- Stress ball

- Stress management
- Subject-related artefacts
- Voice control workshops

 Lightning Ideas

- Discuss the purpose and expectations of your presentation with your tutor
- Check time, location and duration
- Order and check equipment
- Change your group early on if the working relationship is difficult
- Remember strengths, allocate tasks and stick to them
- Remember the accessibility factor
- Copy your slides onto OHPs or a flipchart (a back-up for technical failure)
- Refine your presentation skills by practising often
- Organise therapeutic support
- Place a symbol or colour beside key points on your prompt cards
- Match PowerPoint and prompt card numbers
- Take water and other aids into the presentation room
- Don't fidget
- Hold a pen, if this keeps you calm
- Don't focus on one person only when presenting
- Remember the last minute checklist
- Give handouts – create space for annotation

Prepare well to present well

Please go to the Companion Website for this book www.sagepub.co.uk/gribben to access downloadable resources, all the activities featured here and a podcast for this chapter.

12 Making the Most of Your Feedback

This chapter looks at making the most of your academic feedback so you can become an independent learner. The Consider, Assess and Practise (CAP) feedback process will help you progress in your academic knowledge, develop a deeper understanding of your subject area and acquire the skills needed to demonstrate that knowledge and understanding in your assignments.

| Feedback | Making it personal without taking it personally |

| Step 1: Consider | Step 2: Assess | Step 3: Practise |

| Different feedback methods – same message | Your feedback toolkit | Lightning ideas |

Feedback

Feedback comes in all shapes and sizes. It can be colourful, it can be dull. It can encourage, it can upset. It can boost, it can knock down. It can challenge and even scare. Feedback can affect us in many different ways but knowing what makes feedback good or bad can influence how we make the most of its message.

What makes good feedback 'good'?

Feedback is a learning opportunity that makes what you do meaningful and valuable. It's intended to identify the strengths and weaknesses in your assignments so you can see both the areas you're really good at and the ones you need to work on next time around. It gives pointers to help you improve your researching and writing skills, and so improve your grades. Feedback can be one-off or ongoing, depending on the size of the assignment. If feedback is to enable you to progress in your academic achievements, it should be:

- presented in a clear and understandable manner
- specific to your actual assignment and give you a sense of direction
- positive and constructive with strategies that support your learning
- an opportunity for dialogue between you and the person providing the feedback.

What makes bad feedback 'bad'?

If you come away from your feedback session with more negative than positive feelings then there's something wrong with the feedback presentation. As feedback is a 'look back to feed forward' learning opportunity, it shouldn't be:

- negative
- personally upsetting
- making you feel bad about yourself or denting your confidence
- forcing you to question your abilities to manage your studies.

Making it personal without taking it personally

Feedback is something individual to us all but, really, we shouldn't take it 'personally'. Ever felt it's been personal or felt attacked? Even felt rubbish? Horrible, isn't it? It's meant to help you, they tell us …

Well, try seeing the positive in all that when you've worked your head off, burnt the candle at both ends and been up all night to meet that deadline!

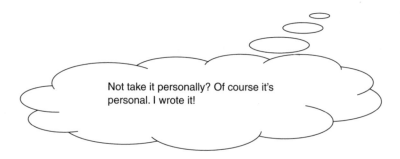

Sure, it's personal to you – it's your blood, sweat and tears, and even your sleepless nights, but the comments and criticism from tutors aren't directed at you personally. They're focused on your work: its content and presentation. So don't let their comments put you off. Don't think of it all as a personal criticism; that's not the intention. Think of it as a new opportunity to learn so you can do things better next time around. Not so sure? Well, stop and think, where are you at right now? Which set of bubbles reflects most closely the way you normally think about feedback?

If it's the bottom set then it's time to remove the Person (your doubting thoughts and feelings) from 'personally' and keep the Ally (your tutor, your peer and their supportive feedback comments). Not quite sure where to start? Why not note how you feel right now. Oh, and don't forget all the positives in your assignment. They're the important confidence builders, and there will be many!

Activity 12.1   Remove the Person, keep the Ally

List what you feel is personal and what's supportive in your feedback

Person	Ally

Now scale your feeling and circle your answer

rubbish   upset   quite unsure   encouraged   more certain   optimistic

Still feeling it's personal? Then take a step back and work your way through the CAP feedback process. If you:

1 Consider – you'll understand how to get rid of the Person and keep the Ally.
2 Assess – you'll learn how to make the most of your feedback message.
3 Practise – you'll develop strategies and methods that support your learning style and learning development.

With some perseverance, you'll soon be swapping the feedback CAP for your graduation cap!

Step 1 – Consider

Waiting to hear back from your first assignment or exam is the scariest thing. It can sometimes feel worse than the actual exam or writing process itself. Will you pass? Will you fail? Was what you wrote good enough? What will the tutor think of your work, of you? These are the thoughts and feelings of every student the world over; no one is exempt. We've all had them at some time or another. The point is you survived the hard work involved in producing an assignment; you even survived the exam pressure, so no doubt you'll survive the feedback too. A few words pointing you in the right direction aren't going to be the end of you. Remember, you can't get everything right first time around. It's all a learning process and you've got to start somewhere. How else will you progress with your study skills and academic writing? How else will you develop your learning processes, improve your understanding, build up your knowledge bank and achieve your goal?

So regardless of the style of feedback you use, the first and most important step is to chat to your tutor and consider the points together. Move beyond the red pen comments, the big empty circles and the many question or exclamation marks. They're just highlighting pointers. Get rid of any personal feelings you have towards your tutor. Put aside your nagging doubts or shaky confidence. Leave your preconceptions at the door and come to the discussion table with an open mind.

 Activity 12.2   Consider the feedback

How do you feel about your feedback? Does it feel more Person or Ally? Start completing your Feedback Face – write down key points to ask your tutor in the thought bubbles. During your meeting, jot down what you need to Stop, Start, Improve and Consider inside the face.

How does it all seem now? Is there more Person or Ally? Has your personal feeling moved or changed? Are you now ready to Assess?

Step 2 – Assess

We've all received comments at one time or another where we've thought: yeah, great feedback but what am I meant to do with all this? How do I know what you mean when you say: Expand here! Expand what, how, where exactly? Then there are all those empty circles with question and exclamation marks – what's that all about?

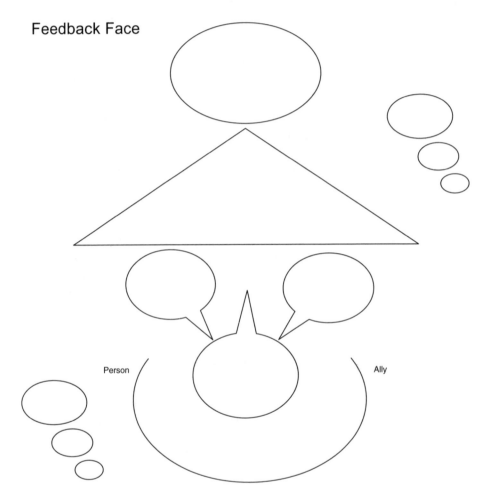

Feedback Face

Person

Ally

Every piece of feedback you're given is meant to raise questions. It's meant to clarify learning outcome expectations versus your actual performance versus any improvement strategies. It's meant to challenge your enquiring mind and test your commitment. Having considered the message behind the feedback comments, you'll reach the point where acknowledging your strengths and weaknesses, your initial thoughts and feelings will help you assess where you're at and what you need to do to improve. Remember, it's what you do with the comments that makes the difference, not simply what they say.

Activity 12.3   From message to feedback

Understood the feedback message? Let's add to your Feedback Face and make a note of what you need to stop, need to start, need to consider and improve upon, and who or what helped. Re-do your scaling; has it changed any? Feel you're starting to remove the Person and keep the Ally?

Step 3 – Practise

Now you've sorted out the comments and know exactly what's been getting in the way, it's time to practise the points you need to work on. Still unsure where to start? Then maybe the examples in Table 12.1 will help.

Table 12.1   Using your feedback

Tutor's comment	What you can do
expand here	list solutions to expand argument
referencing!	practise Harvard referencing exercises
improve your C+ to B with stronger argument	look at other theories or viewpoints to develop your argument
not clear! Where's the discussion going?	check facts and theories; note missing points
more examples here	look for additional examples to support discussion
grammar!	use spell-checker or proofreader
look out for plagiarism! Not your own words	use Turnitin, check sources and write in own words

Did that seem easy enough? Yes! That's not the end of it though. Now you've got the strategy, you need to do something with it. Thinking of your learning style, how would you tackle the task so you can move forward? Think it – note it. Oh, and give yourself a deadline and keep track of when it's done. The 'personally' should seem more distant now.

Activity 12.4   From feedback to strategy

Take comments from your assignment, devise a question, work out the strategy and add to your Feedback Face.

Table 12.2   From comment question to strategy

Point	Questions for your tutor	Strategies
1	What can I do so I don't get marked down for my spelling and grammar? That's my dyslexia, you know!	use a proofreader use a specialist spell-checker
5	You're saying 'look out for plagiarism! that I've not used my own words here.	use Turnitin acknowledge the source re-write in your own words

Different feedback methods – same message

Nowadays, feedback comes in all shapes and sizes, each with opportunities to get feedback on the feedback. The latest technology can provide on-foot feedback – information you can listen to on your MP3 or iPod while moving from point A to B. You can

Activity 12.5   From strategy to action

Task	Action	Deadline	Done (✓)
plagiarism	attend critical thinking classes	_____day / /	
referencing in essays	make index cards of citation styles and how to use these in essays	_____day / /	

even access feedback electronically online to check your progress anytime, anywhere. Or there's the more traditional written feedback style. Regardless of the feedback option, there's something for every type of learner. The way you like to learn will most likely be the way you like to get your feedback. It makes sense! That way, you're guaranteed to make the most of it and that's the big advantage.

Let's be honest though, there may be many advantages, but the small hiccups you meet along the way, such as your tutor's illegible handwriting or the audio file that's too large to download, can sometimes feel like a big disadvantage. Really, it's all a question of tapping into the correct support or resources when you feel stuck. So make sure you know where to go!

Self-assessment feedback journal

Self-assessment is exactly what it says – a personal evaluation of your academic work and progress. It's a slightly different type of feedback, but it's equally valuable. While it may appear less threatening, it can actually be harsher as low confidence can often produce the harshest

 Activity 12.6   Looking back to feed forward

Start your self-assessment journal by developing your own Feedback Face. Remember, it's your own self-assessment, so be honest. Ask yourself:

- how you were able to move beyond the bare comments and empty circles
- who or what helped you acknowledge your feelings and build your confidence
- what enabled you to practise new skills and promote your abilities
- what you can take forward to your next assignment
- what you can Stop, Start, Improve, Consider.

self-critic. Keeping a feedback journal will help you map out where you're at, setting out what you need to stop, start, improve and consider. Creating a journal full of comments, pointers, ideas and strategies from your first to your final year assignment will help support a more confident approach to your honours dissertation or project.

Right, let's get started – see diagram below for examples.

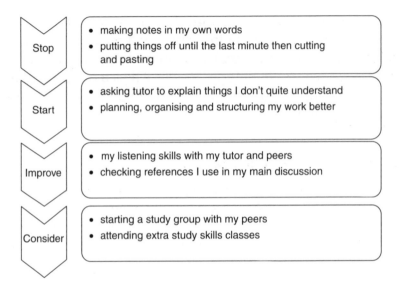

Stop
- making notes in my own words
- putting things off until the last minute then cutting and pasting

Start
- asking tutor to explain things I don't quite understand
- planning, organising and structuring my work better

Improve
- my listening skills with my tutor and peers
- checking references I use in my main discussion

Consider
- starting a study group with my peers
- attending extra study skills classes

Written

Written is very much the type of feedback you'll be used to receiving. You can see the marking criteria, read the comments and identify your strong points and your not so strong ones. A written document gives you space to draw your own red-circle comments and question marks so you come to the discussion table with your tutor feeling prepared. Don't be afraid to ask questions, discuss points, consider strategies, review comments and get clarification so that things can become clearer in your own mind.

Verbal

What about verbal feedback – how useful is that? One great advantage of this is that you can ask as many questions as you need to during your feedback session. Working through points one by one, you can ask for further clarification if things are unclear. By chatting face to face, you'll hear your tutor's comments first hand, witness their tone of voice and body language, and soon understand that the comments aren't at all personally intended. They're purely academic. They're your Ally!

Struggling to remember and jot down more than a few points at a time? Having difficulty understanding the tutor's strange accent? Then why not record the session so you can listen back to the information anytime, anywhere.

Audio

Audio feedback is increasingly becoming more popular as a viable option for receiving tutors' comments about your work. Somehow your feedback seems more personal; you feel tutors seem to engage easier and appear more interested in your work. Download the feedback onto your MP3 player or other recording device and listen on foot, anytime, anywhere.

No problem is too difficult for audio feedback. Even the file that seems too big to download can be accessed through tools such as Audacity, or information emailed through Blackboard. Problem solved!

Online

Let's face it, technology is taking over how we learn; the online course is firmly cemented in education and naturally, therefore, so is online feedback. We just need to work with it to make the feedback work for us. If your tutor uses a podcast or vodcast for feedback, and it suits your learning style, then think of the advantages.

You can:

- book your discussion slot with the tutor
- chat using a webcam
- receive an instant answer in real-time
- probe further so you understand better
- log and save information in a file or on a portable memory stick
- use it as a reference for all future assignments
- review the feedback as often as you like.

Peer

Working on group projects or presentations can sometimes mean group feedback. This can be given face to face as you work on a project or through online discussion rooms, e.g. Moodle. Whatever the approach, remember you're all in the same boat so be honest and be kind. Interaction should be encouraging, supportive, stimulating, motivating and confidence-building. If it's not, then revisit the ground rules and your approach.

Peer feedback lets you :

- define ground rules to express the good, the bad and the ugly in your assignment
- check your progress with others
- take note of body language and tone of voice during webcam or face-to-face discussion
- record information in a group feedback poster for future reference
- arrange real-time discussion through texting.

Your feedback toolkit

Practice makes perfect! The more you develop your skills, the more you develop as a learner. Things don't seem so daunting or difficult when you feel in control of your learning. The feedback toolkit allows you to work through the CAP feedback process while utilising the tools that nurture your learning best.

The visual learner's feedback toolkit

Is it easier if you see a picture of where you need to improve? Then dip into the visual learner's toolkit and create your own visual image. Developing steps for yourself can give you a better understanding of where you've gone wrong, and what you need to prioritise to develop your research and writing skills.

• Academic Poster	• Post-its – shaped, question marks, coloured
• Feedback Face	• Sticky text highlighter strips
• Coloured stickers	• Study Buddies bookmarks
• Highlighters	• Thought bubbles
• Inspiration	

The auditory learner's feedback toolkit

Need to hear where you've gone wrong? Feel you've not heard what was really meant by the comment? Wondered about some miscommunication somewhere along the way? Then dip into the auditory learner's toolkit. Hearing things can help you separate the personal feeling from the constructive criticism, and give you a better understanding.

• Audacity	• Livescribe Echo Pen	• Reflective journal
• Blackboard	• Moodle	• ritePen
• Coloured stickers	• Peer support	• Study skills tutor
• Digital recorder	• Personal tutor	• Traffic Light System

The tactile learner's feedback toolkit

Need to keep on the move so your thoughts and learning keep on the move too? Need to feel the progress? Feel how your learning takes shape? Then dip into the tactile learner's toolkit.

• Academic poster	• Question mark Post-its	• Stress ball
• Arts and crafts toolbox	• Mindfulness exercises	• Study group
• Background music	• SBuddy	• Thought bubbles
• Cardboard	• Sticky text highlighter strips	• Walking mat
• Feedback journal		

Lightning ideas

Consider:

- reading or listening to the comments carefully
- putting your questions in thought bubbles
- asking for clarification and reassurance that you've understood the comments
- using text highlighter coloured stickies
- jotting down a letter, number, symbol or colour to highlight comments you want to discuss
- drawing a large margin at the side of your notes page to annotate any additional comments or strategies you need to adopt
- drawing shapes and bubbles around your feedback face to annotate additional information

Assess:

- reflecting upon the comments you receive
- reading feedback aloud to ensure you've understood
- acknowledging and valuing your efforts
- making a list of specific areas you need to work on
- recording feedback so you can listen anytime, anywhere

Practise:

- exchanging information with your peers
- producing an action plan
- working on the 'weak' areas highlighted in your feedback
- using the comments to improve on your next assignment
- referencing
- writing in your own words

Feedback from the old feeds forward to the new

 Please go to the Companion Website for this book www.sagepub.co.uk/gribben to access downloadable resources, all the activities featured here and a podcast for this chapter.

References

Baddeley, A.D. and Hitch, G.J. (1974) Working memory. In G.H. Bower (ed.) *The Psychology of Learning and Motivation: Advances in Research and Theory.* London: Academic Press Ltd, pp. 47–90.

Bird, R. (2009) *Overcoming Difficulties with Number.* London: Sage Publications.

Burns, T. and Sinfield, S. (2008) *Essential Study Skills: The Complete Guide to Success at University,* 2nd edition: London: Sage Publications.

Field. A. (2009) *Discovering Statistics Using SPSS,* 3rd edition. London: Sage Publications.

Fowler, P. (2000). Cited in Morgan, E. and Klein, C. (2000) *The Dyslexic Adult in a non-dyslexic World.* London: Whurr Publishers, p. 204.

Gathercole, S.E. and Alloway, T.P. (2008) *Working Memory and Learning.* London: Sage Publications.

Gilroy, D.E. and Miles, T.R. (1996) *Dyslexia at College,* 2nd edition. London: Routledge.

Høien-Tengesdal, I. and Tønnessen, F.E. (2011) The relationship between phonological skills and word decoding. *Scandinavian Journal of Psychology,* 52, pp. 93–103.

Judge, B., Jones, P. and McCreery, E. (2009) *Critical Thinking Skills for Education Students.* Exeter: Learning Matters.

Leeds Metropolitan University: Skills for Learning (2009) Quote, Unquote: A guide to Harvard referencing [Internet]. Leeds: Leeds Metropolitan University. Available from: http://skillsforlearning.leedsmet.ac.uk/Quote_Unquote.pdf [Accessed 1 March 2011].

McNeil, F. (2008) *Learning with the Brain in Mind.* London: Sage Publications.

Menter, I. et al. (2010) *A Guide to Practitioner Research in Education.* London: Sage Publications.

Pavey, B., Meehan, M. and Waugh, A. (2010) *Dyslexia-friendly Further and Higher Education.* London: Sage Publications.

Perry, A. (2003) *The Little Book of Procrastination: How to Stop Putting Things Off.* Suffolk: Worth Publishing.

Ridley, D. (2008) *The Literature Review: A Step-by-Step Guide for Students.* London: Sage Publications.

Sambell, K., Gibson, M. and Miller, S. (2010) *Studying Childhood and Early Childhood,* 2nd edition. London: Sage Publications.

Thomas, G. (2009) How to do Your Research Project: *A Guide for Students in Education and Applied Social Sciences.* London: Sage Publications.

Vlachopoulos, P. and Cowan, J. (2010) Choices of approaches in e-moderation: conclusions from a grounded theory study. *Active Learning in Higher Education,* 11(3), pp. 1–13.

Vlachopoulos, P. (2009) Designing flexible programmes: the role of virtual classrooms in enhancing online learning. Virtual paper presented at the Flexible Delivery Symposium, University of Aberdeen, 19–20 May.

Useful Websites

www.1.ibm.com/software/analytics/spss/
www.android.com
www.apple.com/education/itunes-u
www.audionotetaker.com
www.blackboard.com
www.books.google.com
www.camtasia-studio.en.softonic.com
www.claroideas.co.uk
www.clarosoftware.com
www.dabbleboard.com
www.endnote.com
www.evernote.com
www.exploratree.org.uk
http://audacity.sourceforge.net
http://bubbl.us
http://moodle.org
www.inspiration.com
www.learning-styles-online.com
www.livescribe.com
www.matchware.com
www.mindfulness.com
www.mindgenius.com
www.mindjet.com
www.mindmappingmac.com

www.mindmeister.com
www.mywebspiration.com
www.olympus.co.uk/voice
www.nuance.com
www.nova.edu/library/help/misc/dewey.html
www.nova.edu/library/help/misc/libraryofcongress.html
www.podbean.com
www.ritescript.com
www.rsc-ne.scotland.org.uk
www.sbuddy.co.uk
www.scholar.google.co.uk
www.skype.com
www.smartsheet.com
www.texthelp.com
www.topicscape.com
www.turnitin.com
www.twitter.com
www.webopedia.com
www.weightworld.co.uk/wobble-board
www.wisemapping.com
www.zotero.org

Index

Added to a page number 'f' denotes a figure and 't' denotes a table.